and then shall the end come...

A concise, chronological guide to fully understanding the end times

JOHN R. BISAGNO

Houston, Texas

2000

Dr. John R. Bisagno
P. O. Box 79721
Houston, TX 77279-9721

Book design by Rita Mills
Cover Design by Scott A. Reavis

ISBN Number 0-9666595-9-7

Printed in the United States of America

Table of Contents

Preface

I am often asked whether we are living in the last days. It seems people everywhere have an unsettling sense that something is about to occur, but really don't know what it is. This question is most often accompanied by fear and concern. Invariably, when a serious newsstory unfolds in the Middle East, I get phone calls from people asking if the situation will escalate into the battle of Armageddon, and naturally, they are afraid. There was a time not long ago when serious news-making events were few and far between. We gathered around our television sets with great anxiety, watching and wondering what the world was coming to. Now hardly a day passes without something newsworthy happening somewhere in the world. However, today, in our desensitization, we shake our heads in despair and no longer question what the world is coming to, but how it can possibly go on.

What is happening? Why is there still no peace on earth? Why are false Messiahs popping up everywhere? Why has our weather gone berserk? And why is El Nino blamed for every weather calamity on earth when most people had never heard of it prior to the '90s? We will discover the answers to these questions and many more as we turn to Scripture, the only reliable Truth. What is happening in our world today was foretold thousands of years ago, and despite assertions to the contrary, the Word of God really does provide a detailed road map of what lies just around the corner.

I am thrilled to tell you, as believers, we are the generation who will see the return of Christ. While we can expect the conditions on earth to steadily worsen, we have the blessed assurance of being spared the coming Tribulation. The world in all its chaos and wickedness would have us believe there is no God, or at least He is not in control. But our God is living and sovereign, and they simply fail to see what is happening in the world today is in prophetic fulfillment of His Word. I urge you to "...stand firm and hold to the traditions which we were taught..." (2 Thess. 2:15), "...so that when He appears, we may have confidence and not shrink away from Him in shame at His coming" (1 John 2:28).

For those who have not trusted in Jesus as Lord and Savior, time is running out. The Bible tells us, "The wages of sin is death, but the free gift of God is eternal life in Christ Jesus our Lord" (Rom. 6:23). Nearly 2,000 years ago, God came into the world in the form of a man, Jesus Christ, to pay the price for sin. In His infinite love for all of us, no matter who you are or what you have done, He willingly placed our sin on Himself and died so that we may live eternally. Because God is holy and we are born with a sin nature, we cannot come into His presence unless our sin is atoned for, and that is exactly what Jesus did on the cross. Placing our trust in Him as Lord and Savior enables us to get to God. Jesus assured us, "I am the Way, and the Truth, and the Life; no one comes to the Father, but through Me" (John 14:6).

Salvation is freely given to everyone who acknowledges this truth and believes in their heart God raised Him from the dead. By placing your trust in Jesus, you are completely forgiven of every sin you have ever committed or will commit in the future. They are remembered no more, ever.

We are promised, "As far as the east is from the west, so far has He removed our transgressions from us" (Ps. 103:12), and "through His name everyone who believes in Him receives forgiveness of sins" (Acts 10:43). But the time is drawing near when tremendous persecution and certain death will accompany salvation. I plead with you to delay no longer in asking Jesus to come into your heart. In so doing, you too will be spared the coming Tribulation, and moreover, eternal separation from God.

With prophecy unfolding at an unprecedented rate and the "signs of the times" frequently occurring, I write these words of truth and hope for believers everywhere awaiting the return of Christ. Indeed, Jesus is coming to receive His Bride unto Himself, and we should have exciting tranquility in our hearts in the midst of all the worldly chaos we are experiencing. Scripture warns us of what is happening today and what we can expect of tomorrow.

It is my prayer that all who read this writing will lay aside any doubt or skepticism and open your hearts and minds to the truth of God's Word. His truth is not based on whether we believe; but rather, we believe because it is based on truth.

Dr. John R. Bisagno

If anyone has an ear, let him hear.

Revelation 13:9

Know this first of all, that in the last days mockers will come with their mocking, following after their own lusts, and saying, 'Where is the promise of His coming? For ever since the fathers fell asleep, all continues just as it was from the beginning of creation.'

2 Peter 3:3-4

Introduction

One can hardly turn on a Christian radio or television broadcast without hearing someone talk about the end times in which we are living. Nearly 3,000 years ago, the prophet Amos wrote, "Surely the Lord God does nothing unless He reveals His secret counsel to His servants the prophets" (Amos 3:7). God has impressed on the hearts of spiritual leaders everywhere an urgency to deliver the message that Jesus is coming, and come He must. The Second Coming of Christ is the central event toward which all of history is moving and without which none of history makes any sense.

Over the last thirty years, countless books, magazines, and newspaper articles have been written on prophecy. Unfortunately, those who foolishly set dates and times for the return of Christ have only served to cause confusion. As each of those dates came and went, excitement turned to skepticism to the point that today most nonbelievers, and even a host of believers, give little regard, oftentimes scoffing, when mention is made of Christ's imminent return. This very mockery is in fulfillment of the apostle Peter's prophetic words written over 1900 years ago: "Know this first of all, that in the last days mockers will come with their mocking, following after their own lusts, and saying, 'Where is the promise of His coming? For ever since the fathers fell asleep, all continues just as it was from the beginning of creation'" (2 Pet. 3:3-4).

Adding to the confusion are the well-intentioned, yet misguided individuals who have offered incorrect interpretations of Scripture, basing their positions on a single verse rather than applying the Scriptures as a whole. As a result, theories and speculations abound, and unless someone has a passion to perform the in-depth study required in order to fully understand what God's Word says about end-time prophecy, most are left to wonder who is actually right in their individual interpretations. Peter wrote, "Some things (are) hard to understand, which the untaught and unstable distort" (2 Pet. 3:16).

I can only hope this book will clear up a lot of the confusion. Scores of resources are available to anyone who wishes to know the various viewpoints regarding end-time prophecy. I will not endeavor to expound on them since they are of no significance to the material contained in this writing.

I espouse a full, pre-Tribulation Rapture viewpoint, a complete seven-year Tribulation period, followed by the 1000-year millennial reign of Christ. To many, these terms may be unclear at this point, but as we progress, explanation will be given of their meaning and where they are supported in the Scriptures.

Indeed, God's Word reveals end-time prophecy with

amazing attention to detail. My purpose in writing is to provide a clear understanding of these prophecies, placing them in their chronological order beginning with the signs of the times of which Jesus warned, followed by the Rapture of the Church, and including everything in between to the New Jerusalem, which will descend out of heaven to a newly created earth where believers will live for eternity.

When the Tribulation begins, prophecy will unfold rapidly. "For the Lord will execute His Word upon the earth, thoroughly and quickly" (Rom. 9:28). Many of these prophecies will occur simultaneously. As such, it will be noted when these events overlap. While current events substantiate that we are living in the last days and must therefore be included in any book on prophecy, this writing will not center around today's newsmakers, but rather, in light of today's unsettling events, what God's Word says is going to happen next.

> *All scripture is inspired by God and profitable for teaching, for reproof, for correction, for training in righteousness; that the man of God may be adequate, equipped for every good work.*
>
> 2 Timothy 3:16-17

Chapter 1

The Authenticity of The Bible

Can we really trust what the Bible says, or is it full of errors and contradictions? A person's willingness to accept the truth of God's Word is related to their willingness to receive its Author. Usually those who attack the authenticity of the Bible are the very ones refusing to subject their lives to its authority. Most scoffers have never read the Bible, but instead have adopted the views of critics who discount it with ever-popular gems like, "It's something written by men, so it's full of errors," or, "Everyone has a different interpretation of the Bible."

Someone once said, "Sin keeps a person from reading the Bible, and reading the Bible keeps a person from sin."

The fact of the matter is, the Bible convicts man's heart of sin, and rather than coming into agreement with God over our sinful ways and turning from them, many prefer the darkness over the light and deny the validity of the Bible so they may live as they please. We are assured, "In the last time there shall be mockers, following after their own ungodly lusts. These are the ones who cause divisions, (are) worldly-minded, devoid of the Spirit" (Jude 18-19).

At no other time in its history has the Bible been under so much attack. Yet those who are driven with discrediting God's Word are simply in keeping with their very nature. The apostle Paul warned us that unbelievers "do not accept the things of the Spirit of God; for they are foolishness to him, and he cannot understand them, because they are spiritually appraised" (1 Cor. 2:14). He further added, "The god of this world (Satan) has blinded the minds of the unbelieving, that they might not see the light of the gospel of the glory of Christ" (2 Cor. 4:4, parentheses mine).

In fact, it is the work of the Holy Spirit who "guides us into all the truth" (John 16:13), and when He comes to live in us, it is He who "opens our minds to understand the Scriptures" (Luke 24:45). In His high priestly prayer to the Father the night before He was crucified, Jesus included these words on behalf of all believers: "Sanctify them in the truth; Thy Word is truth" (John 17:17).

Unbelievers cannot comprehend the Scriptures, and by denying the authenticity of the Bible, they consequently believe they are under no obligation to abide by its authority. In making the claims of interpretation issues or errors made by man in its translation, they necessarily influence the hearts and minds of others, who unwittingly adopt the same beliefs and spread these untruths without even bothering to open the Bible to see what it says for themselves. As a result, sin has become so prevalent in society, that those who choose to obey God's Word and live under its authority are viewed as narrow-minded and intolerant, often the target of ridicule. Scripture is clear: "Anyone who goes too far and does not abide in the teaching of Christ, does not have God" (2 John 1:9).

No other book has been banned, burned, or hated more than the Bible, yet it continues to outsell all other books. It is currently available, in whole or in part, in over 1100 languages and dialects. Many of these languages were reduced to writing solely in order that the Bible may be translated into their written format.[1] Over the centuries, countless men and women have died defending its truth, and Christians today have no less a responsibility in preserving its honor and authority as the Word of God.

Unfortunately, when believers are confronted with unfounded denial of the Bible's authenticity, many are ill-prepared to respond in its defense and usually feel defeated, wishing they knew what to say when the situation comes up again, or worse, avoiding the situation altogether. I encourage you to read *Why I Believe* by pastor and author D. James Kennedy. His excellent book provides compelling and irrefutable evidence of the authenticity of God's Word, equipping the believer with a response to every objection he may hear.

The Bible was written by some forty different authors who were inspired by the Holy Spirit. It was written over a 1500-year period in the Hebrew, Aramaic, and Greek languages. These authors were spread over the continents of Asia, Africa, and Europe with backgrounds ranging from fishermen to kings. Matthew was a tax collector. David was a shepherd. Paul was a rabbi and tent maker. Luke was a physician. Daniel was a prime minister. Peter, James, and John were fishermen. Amos was a farmer. Solomon was a king. Jeremiah, Ezekiel, and Zechariah were all priests. Most of these authors never even met each other, yet they all consistently wrote of a common theme, the redemption of mankind through the Lord Jesus Christ.

When we consider the possibility of this occurring, we are left to conclude there is no way this could be done unless it were written by God. If I were to select ten people from all walks of life and ask them to write a story on a common theme, without telling them the theme, of course I would receive ten papers with ten different themes. Even if I told the same ten people a story with its theme and then asked them to write a paper on it, there is no doubt I would receive ten different versions of how they perceived the story.

Despite the astounding fact of the Bible's consistent theme as recorded by forty different authors, there will nonetheless be skeptics who claim these authors read one another's writings, copying each other's works. But this view is wholly without basis and ignores indisputable evidence to the contrary.

People have also been brainwashed into believing science has disproven the Bible. In fact, science confirms the validity of Scripture. Sir Cecil Wakeley, one of the world's leading scientists, has said, "Scripture is quite definite that God created the world, and I for one believe that to be a fact, not fiction."[2] Millions of people the world over passionately cling to the Theory of Evolution without even realizing that many of those who originally espoused it ultimately abandoned their beliefs. In fact, Charles Darwin himself said, "The distinctions of specific forms and their not being blended together by innumerable transitional links is a very obvious difficulty."[3]

T. H. Morgan, an outspoken evolutionist, is quoted as saying, "Within the period of human history we do not know of a single instance of the transformation of one species into another.... It may be claimed that the theory of descent is lacking, therefore, in the most essential feature that it needs to place the theory on a scientific basis. This must be admitted."[4]

As well, Sir Julian Huxley, one of the world's leading evolutionists and descendant of Thomas Huxley, an ardent colleague and follower of Charles Darwin stated, "I suppose the reason we leaped at The Origin of Species was because the idea of God interfered with our sexual mores."[5]

Again, British evolutionist Sir Arthur Keith has said, "Evolution is unproved and unprovable. We believe it because the only alternative is special creation, which is unthinkable."[6]

Finally, physicist H. J. Lipson once stated, "I think however that we must go further than this and admit that the only acceptable explanation is Creation. I know that this is anathema to physicists, as indeed it is to me, but we must not reject a theory that we do not like if the experimental evidence supports it."[7]

I am always left to wonder why people are so willing to believe what so-called individuals of higher learning tell us when God's Word tells us otherwise. The apostle Paul wrote, "The wisdom of this world is foolishness before God" (1 Cor. 3:19), and, "The Lord knows the reasonings of the wise, that they are useless" (1 Cor. 3:20). Of course, we accept the world's words as truth because as laymen, we have no way of confirming what we are told.

For years, scientists told us the planet Saturn had seven rings. Of course we believed it. Why wouldn't we? They had the telescopes to confirm it. But it was not until the recent development of further space technology, enabling us to get a closer look at distant planets, that scientists were able to determine that Saturn, in fact, has a myriad of rings. Indeed, an in-depth study of the planetary system alone will convince the hardest skeptic of the existence of God. David wrote, "The heavens are telling of the glory of God; and their expanse is declaring the work of His hands" (Ps. 19:1).

So while we may depend on scientists to enlighten us in scientific matters, when it comes to spiritual matters, we must realize that many of these learned individuals are unbelievers and their opinions are tempered with the human perspective. Without question, where science and Scripture appear to conflict, we must always defer to God's Word as truth over the reasonings of man, for "it is better to take refuge in the Lord than to trust in man" (Ps. 118:8). The apostle Paul wrote, "Your faith should not rest on the wisdom of men" (1 Cor. 2:5).

Finally, the Bible has been undeniably authenticated through archaeological finds. There have been over 25,000 archaeological discoveries pertaining to the Bible, as well as tens of thousands of confirmed records regarding individuals and events recorded in the Bible.[8] Jewish archaeologist Nelson Glueck has said, "It may be stated categorically that no archaeological discovery has ever controverted a biblical reference."[9]

In 1977, Major General Chaim Herzog, former Israeli Ambassador to the United Nations, was quoted as saying, "Everywhere you turn in Israel today the Bible is coming to life. I'm not talking only about archaeological discoveries, but about the international political scene as it affects us today. If you read the biblical prophecies about Armageddon and the end days, and you look at the current realities in the world and especially in the Middle East, things certainly begin to look familiar. The vast number of archaeological discoveries in Israel have all tended to vindicate the pictures that are presented in the Bible. If therefore the Bible has been proven true concerning the past, we cannot look lightly at any prognostication it makes about the future."[10]

So can we trust what the Bible tells us? Indeed we can. Is it full of errors and contradictions? No way.

> *May Thy loving kindnesses also come to me, O Lord, Thy salvation according to Thy Word; so I shall have an answer for him who reproaches me, for I trust in Thy Word.*
>
> Psalm 119:41-42

Endnotes

1) Steven Barabas, Th.D., (Princeton Theological Seminary), Professor of Theology, Wheaton College, Author: *So Great Salvation.*
2) Quoted in D. James Kennedy, *Why I Believe* (Word Publishing, 1980), p. 52.
3) Creation-Evolution Encyclopedia, "Origin of the Species Unknown," Creation Science Facts.
4) Quoted in D. James Kennedy, *Why I Believe* (Word Publishing, 1980), p. 59.
5) Ibid., p. 52.
6) Ibid., p. 51.
7) Creation-Evolution Encyclopedia, "Origin of the Species Unknown," Creation Science Facts.
8) D. James Kennedy, *Why I Believe* (Word Publishing, 1980), p. 35.
9) Ibid., p. 36.
10) Hal Lindsey, *The 1980's: Countdown to Armageddon* (Bantam Books, New York, 1980), p. 35.

> *Know this first of all that no prophecy of Scripture is a matter of one's own interpretation, for no prophecy was ever made by an act of human will, but men moved by the Holy Spirit spoke from God.*
>
> 2 Peter 1:20-21

Chapter 2

Prophecy in The Bible

We live in an age of psychics and soothsayers, telling hopeful listeners what they want to hear regarding their future. God's Word is very clear about those who profess this ability, as well as those seeking direction from them. Moses warned the children of God, "There shall not be found among you...one who uses divination, one who practices witchcraft, or one who interprets omens, or a sorcerer, or one who casts a spell, or a medium, or a spiritist, or one who calls up the dead. For whoever does these things is detestable to the Lord...for (the) nations...listen to those who practice witchcraft and to diviners, but as for you, the Lord your God has not allowed you to do so" (Deut. 18:10-12).

Even though this instruction was given to the Israelites thousands of years ago, it still applies to believers today because the Bible tells us God is the same yesterday, today, and forever (Heb. 13:8), and that He changes not (Mal. 3:6).

Though society changes, God remains the same, and we are never left to wonder where He stands on any given issue when it is written in His Word.

Christians are forbidden to seek clairvoyant guidance. It is not for us to know what will happen in our individual future. We are to depend solely on the provision of God and only seek answers to our questions through prayer and abiding in His Word for the direction we need in our everyday lives. All God wants us to know about the future is how it pertains to mankind as a whole, and just as all biblical prophecy up to now has been fulfilled with 100% accuracy, so will be that which remains.

So what about all these psychics who possess the intriguing ability to see into the future, such as Nostradamus, Edgar Cayce, or Jeane Dixon? Doctors and scientists tell us we only use ten percent of our brain capacity, so perhaps the answer lies in their greater command of brain function. That may be, but I am more inclined to believe what the apostle Paul wrote. "The Spirit explicitly says that in later times some will fall away from the faith, paying attention to deceitful spirits and doctrines of demons" (1 Tim. 4:1). In her book The Beautiful Side of Evil, Johanna Michaelsen reveals her own 14-month experience as an assistant to a psychic surgeon and how God showed her that the incredible healings she witnessed were directly attributed to evil shrouded in holiness.[1]

God's Word gives us the standard by which a prophet must be measured. Moses warned us how we could know for sure if those telling the future are from God. "When a prophet speaks in the name of the Lord, if the thing does not come about or come true, that is the thing which the Lord has not spoken" (Deut. 18:22). In fact, if the prophecy does not come true, God's Word assures us, "The prophet has spoken it presumptuously" (Deut. 18:22), meaning "overstepping due bounds" or "taking liberties," as Webster defines it.

And what of the channelers who claim to be talking to the departed? There certainly exists the spirit realm where Satan, the god of this world, rules. When a person foolishly elects to communicate with the spirits through the use of Ouija boards or seances, they are dealing with evil darkness, and are as such, vulnerable to demonic forces of deception. The apostle Paul assures the believer, "To be absent from the body is to be at home with the Lord" (2 Cor. 5:8), not roaming around in some spiritual state waiting for someone to do something on our behalf so we may be released to our eternal abodes. And further, when anyone dies, their souls do not return to take up residence in another person's body. Scripture clearly states: "It is appointed for men to die once and after this comes judgment" (Heb. 9:27, emphasis mine). In the case of Lazarus (John 11:1-46), the widow of Nain's son (Luke 7:11-17), the synagogue official's daughter (Matt. 9:18-25), the disciple Tabitha (Acts 9:36-41), Eutychus, who fell from a third-floor window (Acts 20:9-10), and all the saints who came forth from their graves at Christ's resurrection (Matt. 27:52-53), in every single case, the miracle of bringing them back to life was permitted by God as a witness of His power and to bring glory unto Himself. So there is a dark mystery to all the psychic phenomena, but it bears no relation to the light and goodness of God. Indeed, "God is light, and in Him there is no darkness at all" (1 John 1:5).

It is interesting to note those who claim to have the uncanny ability to see into the future never state dates and times or scores of ballgames or anything near a specific prediction. Instead, they make broad predictions based on the odds of an event taking place. A psychic may state a plane will crash within the year, but they will not give the airline, the date, or any other specific information so we can all stay off that plane. I am certainly not clairvoyant, but with the congestion in airline traffic, our aging planes, the certainty of human error, and a number of other factors, even I can predict a plane will go down in the near future. Consequently, when the tragedy does occur, the psychic is touted as capable of telling the future, and proceeds to make a handsome living off of confused and desperate people in search of answers.

The CSICOP, Committee for the Scientific Investigation of Claims of the Paranormal, a nonprofit scientific and educational organization formed eighteen years ago, objectively examines claims of psychic or paranormal activity and publishes the results of their findings in a magazine entitled Skeptical Inquirer. Eugene Emery of CSICOP compiled a list of predictions from the top psychics of tabloid magazines such as *The National Enquirer, The Sun, The Globe,* and *The National Examiner.* Here are just a few predictions they had for 1996.

- While giving testimony in the civil suit, O. J. Simpson will confess to killing Nicole Brown Simpson and Ronald Goldman, and then become a minister.
- Middle East terrorists will kidnap Barbara Walters and free her after ABC gives them a three-hour platform to express their views, hosted by Barbara, of course.
- Michael Jackson will have a sex-change operation, insisting everyone refer to him as Michelle, while wife, Lisa Marie, stands by her man.

- Susan Lucci will win an Emmy but break a toe after dropping it on her foot.[2]

While these predictions are certainly amusing, not one of them came true. In fact, the accuracy rating of all psychics falls miserably short of perfection. Nationally renowned psychic Sylvia Browne, who has made the rounds on the talk-show circuit, chooses her words a little more carefully, but also missed the mark of perfection in her predictions for 1997. Here are just a few.

- A commercial airline leaving Egypt could be at risk of a bomb in April.
- Tornadoes in great number will devastate parts of Oklahoma, Kansas, and Missouri in April.
- Barbra Streisand will marry an actor. (She married actor James Brolin in 1998.)
- Hillary Rodham Clinton will be exposed in a scandalous long-time affair.[3]

Despite her inaccuracies, Ms. Browne has felt confident enough to map out mankind's future for the next 100 years. Among her forty predictions, she foresees the following:

- Houses will be constructed with a third floor and a rollback roof to allow Hovercrafts the ability to come and go.
- Atlantis will slowly resurface around 2023 and become fully visible by 2026.
- The West Coast will *finally* fall into the ocean in 2026.
- Aliens will show themselves in the year 2010, not to harm us, but to see what we are doing to the earth and then reacquaint us with the anti-gravity devices we used to construct

the pyramids.

- Peace will come in the year 2050 and last for fifty years until 2100 (when she fails to see anything beyond, attributing that to "the end will come like a thief in the night").
- No world war, no nuclear holocaust, just little skirmishes.[4]

In 1552, French physician and highly acclaimed psychic Michael Nostradamus predicted the end of the world would come in 3747. That would be 1,647 years later than Ms. Browne's prediction, and that presents a problem. So whom shall we believe? Neither.

As we shall see, God's Word predicts a far different future for mankind, providing graphic and specific detail. And incidentally, He tells us there will be *no* real peace until Jesus returns to the earth, and, yes, all the nations of the world *will* come together in a final nuclear holocaust.

The Bible is God-breathed, His spoken Word to mankind. Over 3800 times, the Bible says, "Thus saith the Lord," "The Word of God," or "The Word of the Lord." Jesus said, "The Spirit of truth...will guide you into all the truth; for He will not speak on His own initiative, but whatever He hears, He will speak; and He will disclose to you what is to come" (John 16:13). That is why thousands of prophecies have been fulfilled with complete accuracy. This fact alone points to the undeniable truth and sovereignty of God. Outside of the prophetical Scriptures, without fail, no one has predicted the future with accuracy. Only God is able to do so, and tells us that in His Word. "Remember the former things long past, for I am God, and there is no one like Me, declaring the end from the beginning and from ancient times things which have not been done.... Truly I have spoken; truly I will bring it to pass. I have planned it, surely I will do it"

(Isa. 46:9-11).

Nearly one-third of the Bible relates to prophecy. In the Old Testament alone, over 2,000 prophecies have already been fulfilled,[5] of which more than 300 pertain to the birth, life, ministry, death, and resurrection of Jesus. Nearly a thousand years before its fulfillment, David relates his own struggle with death to what Jesus would eventually suffer. "A band of evildoers has encompassed me; they pierced my hands and my feet. They divide my garments among them, and for my clothing they cast lots" (Ps. 22:16, 18). Incredibly, David is describing death by crucifixion, a Roman method of execution not to be introduced for another 700 years.

Of course, I encourage you to read the Scriptures daily and discover for yourself the rich treasure of God's Word. As you learn of prophecy and its fulfillment, you will be blessed with a renewed sense of trust in the faithfulness of God to do just as He promises.

The prophets in the Bible are referred to as major and minor prophets. The minor prophets are certainly of equal stature to the major prophets, only their writings are not as long. In the Old Testament, the Hebrew words *navi', ro'eh,* and *hozeh* all refer to a "spokesman of God." Their function as prophets is clearly stated. God says, "I will raise up a prophet...and I will put My words in his mouth, and he shall speak to them all that I command him" (Deut. 18:18). Here are just a few Old Testament prophecies from Isaiah, a major prophet, and Zechariah, a minor prophet, and where their fulfillment is found in the New Testament. Incidentally, *all* of the Bible's prophets had something to say about the world we live in today.

Referred to as "the evangelical prophet," Isaiah spoke

continually of the redemptive work of Christ some 700 years before His incarnation. Interestingly, the name Isaiah means "Salvation of Jehovah." Starting in 740 B.C., Isaiah's public ministry spanned a period of sixty years until his death at 120 years of age. He recorded many prophecies regarding the life of Christ.

Isaiah 7:14

> *Therefore the Lord Himself will give you a sign: Behold, a virgin will be with child and bear a son, and she will call His name Immanuel.*

Matthew 1:18-25

> *Now the birth of Jesus Christ was as follows. When His mother Mary had been betrothed to Joseph, before they came together she was found to be with child by the Holy Spirit.... And she will bear a Son...and they shall call His name Immanuel, which translated means God With Us....*

Isaiah 53:4-5

> *Surely our griefs He Himself bore, and our sorrows He carried; yet we ourselves esteemed Him stricken, smitten of God, and afflicted. But He was pierced through for our transgressions, He was crushed for our iniquities; the chastening for our well-being fell upon Him, and by His scourging we are healed.*

Matthew 8:16

> *...they brought to Him many who were demon-possessed; and He cast out the spirits with a word, and healed all who were ill.*

John 19:34

One of the soldiers pierced His side with a spear....

John 19:1

Then Pilate therefore took Jesus and scourged Him.

Isaiah 53:7

He was oppressed and He was afflicted, yet He did not open His mouth; like a lamb that is led to slaughter, and like a sheep that is silent before its shearers, so He did not open His mouth.

Matthew 27:12-14

And while He was being accused by the chief priests and elders, He made no answer. Then Pilate said to Him, 'Do You not hear how many things they testify against You?' And He did not answer him with regard to even a single charge, so that the governor was quite amazed.

Isaiah 50:6

I gave My back to those who strike Me, and My cheeks to those who pluck out the beard; I did not cover My face from humiliation and spitting.

Matthew 26:67

Then they spat in His face and beat Him with their fists; and others slapped Him.

Isaiah 40:3

A voice is calling, clear the way for the Lord in the wilderness; make smooth in the desert a highway for our God.

Matthew 3:1-2

John the Baptist came, preaching in the wilderness of Judea, saying, 'Repent, for the kingdom of heaven is at hand.'

Zechariah was a priest and an exile in the Babylonian captivitiy. He was called to be a prophet in 520 B.C. Zechariah means "The Lord Remembers." Accordingly, the theme of his writing regarded the coming of the Messiah and the restoration of Israel.

Zechariah 11:12-13

'If it is good in your sight, give me my wages; but if not, never mind!' So they weighed out thirty shekels of silver as my wages. Then the Lord said to me, 'Throw it to the potter, that magnificent price at which I was valued by them.' So I took the thirty shekels of silver and threw them to the potter in the house of the Lord.

Matthew 26:14-15

Judas Iscariot went to the chief priests and said, 'What are you willing to give me to deliver Him up to you?' And they weighed out to him thirty pieces of silver.

Matthew 27:5, 7

And he threw the pieces of silver into the sanctuary and departed...and they counseled together and with the money bought the Potter's Field as a burial place for strangers.

Zechariah 9:9

...Behold, your king is coming to you; He is just and

endowed with salvation, humble and mounted on a donkey, even on a colt, the foal of a donkey.

Luke 19:30, 35

Go into the village...you will find a colt tied, on which no one yet has ever sat...bring it here. And they brought it to Jesus, and they threw their garments on the colt, and put Jesus on it.

Zechariah 13:7

...Strike the Shepherd that the sheep may be scattered....

Matthew 26:55-56

'...Have you come out with swords and clubs to arrest Me as against a robber?'...Then all the disciples left Him and fled.

Of course, one may shrug his shoulders and suggest the fulfillment of these prophecies is mere coincidence, but the statistical probability of just these eight prophecies alone being fulfilled is one in ten to the seventeenth power, that is, one in 100,000,000,000,000,000 chances. When we consider more than 2,000 others have already been fulfilled, the odds become incalculable. The odds of these eight prophecies being fulfilled in the life of one Man are equivalent to filling the entire state of Texas knee-deep with quarters, then someone flying overhead in a plane and dropping a dime into the pile, the quarters then being mixed and shuffled for two years, and a blindfolded man finding the dime on his first try.

The fulfillment of thousands of prophecies alone provides more than convincing proof that we can believe the Bible and trust its Author. At this pivotal time in history, there remain no other prophecies to be fulfilled except those pertaining to the end times, and they will be fulfilled as well. Jesus said, "Truly I say to you, until heaven and earth pass away, not the smallest letter or stroke shall pass away from the Law, until all is accomplished" (Matt. 5:18). History is a record of events after they happen. Anyone can write history. Prophecy is a record of events before they happen, and none but God can write prophecy.

> *I am watching over My word to perform it.*
>
> Jeremiah 1:12

Endnotes

1) Johanna Michaelsen, *The Beautiful Side of Evil* (Harvest House Publishers, Eugene, Oregon, 1982).
2) Eugene Emery, CSICOP Press Release, December 1996.
3) Sylvia Browne, "1997 Predictions by Sylvia Browne," October 19, 1996, Sylvia Browne Corporation.
4) Sylvia Browne, "Predictions for the Next Hundred Years," April 1997, Sylvia Browne Corporation.
5) D. James Kennedy, *Why I Believe* (Word Publishing, 1980), page 26.

> *...Do you know how to discern the appearance of the sky, but cannot discern the signs of the times?*
>
> Matthew 16:3

Chapter 3

Signs of the Times

After chastising the scribes and Pharisees for their hypocrisy, Jesus left the Temple and began walking toward the Mount of Olives just east of Jerusalem. The disciples followed along, and while crossing the Kidron Valley, hoped to lighten the mood of things by pointing out to Jesus the beauty of all the Temple buildings. He responded with prophecy, telling them all the buildings would be totally destroyed, "not one stone left upon another" (Matt. 24:2). When He reached His destination on the Mount, He sat down and the disciples gathered around. They began asking a series of questions regarding what He had told them along the way. They said, "Tell us, when will these things be, and what will be the sign of Your coming, and of the end of the age?" (Matt. 24:3)

Jesus revealed the answers to two of their questions in His apocalyptic sermon known today as the Olivet Discourse. The one question Jesus did not answer was when the Temple would be destroyed. Instead, His prophetic words were fulfilled approximately forty years later in 70 A.D. when the Roman general Titus conquered Jerusalem and completely destroyed it.

In the Olivet Discourse, Jesus revealed a number of signs to determine "the end of the age." Of course, any of the signs can be identified throughout history as isolated events here and there, but the *simultaneous* occurrence of the signs, combined with their frequency and intensity, depicts the benchmark to precede Christ's return. Jesus related the signs to birth pains (Matt. 24:8). When a woman is about to give birth, she experiences painful contractions which increase in frequency and intensity the closer she is to delivering her child. Just so, the closer we get to the return of Christ, the more frequent and intense the signs will become.

After announcing the "signs of the times" which precede His return, Jesus gave the parable of the fig tree. The fig tree is symbolic of Israel. He said, "When its branch has already become tender, and puts forth its leaves, you know that summer is near; even so you too, when you see all these things, recognize that He is near, right at the door" (Matt. 24:32-33). He added, "Truly I say to you, this generation will not pass away until all these things take place" (Matt. 24:34).

Since the day Jesus ascended to the Father, Christians have been watching the skies for His return. Over the centuries, strange or unusual occurrences often triggered apocalyptic fervor, causing the uninformed to run around like Chicken Little, saying, "The end is near! The end is near!" Because of it, we are experiencing a "little-boy-who-cried-wolf syndrome" where few are listening anymore, when it really is the truth. And now that the new Millennium has caught the attention of Hollywood, the seriousness of these end times has been relegated to mere sensational entertainment to scare its audiences, while seldom bearing any resemblance to the truth. The media has also done its share of diffusing all the end-time clamor by relating it to the same hoopla surrounding the turn of the Millennium.

Though all the doomsdayers of old meant well, the fact is, the countdown to the end times could not even begin until a single event took place; the statehood of Israel. As the fig tree, Israel "became tender" on May 14, 1948. On that date, after some 1900 years without a homeland, the Jews reunited to form the nation of Israel. This was a miracle of untold proportion. At no other time in history has a country ceased to completely exist and then later revive to form a nation. Mark Twain once said, "All things are mortal but the Jew; all other forces pass, but he remains. What is the secret of his immortality?"[1] The Jews continue to exist because God has a plan for them, and it centers around a covenant He made with Abraham over 4,000 years ago.

During His Olivet Discourse, Jesus likened the attitude of the generation who would witness His return to the apathy of Noah's days when Noah warned the people of the impending flood, but "they did not understand until the flood came and took them all away" (Matt. 24:39). Despite 120 years of warning beforehand, the people ignored Noah, laughing and ridiculing him as he constructed the ark and gathered the animals in by twos. After all, it had never rained on the earth up to that point, so obviously he must have been a lunatic. When the time came for Noah and his family to enter the ark, God closed the door behind them, and all the laughing and ridicule came to an end (*see* Gen. 6-7).

Just so today, despite all the words of warning, our apathetic generation simply will not take heed. Scripture speaks to this: "Behold, you scoffers, and marvel, and perish; for I am accomplishing a work in your days, a work which you will never believe, though someone should describe it to you" (Acts 13:41). Like Noah, believers who proclaim Jesus is coming are oftentimes viewed as weirdos or lunatics, and we are left to carry the burden of the nonbelievers' fate, just as Noah and his family anguished over everyone outside the ark. As the unfamiliar rains descended and the waters rose, they likely pounded on the ark, begging to get in, all the while facing the sickening realization that his warnings had actually come true. And so it will be for all who have heard and chosen to ignore the warnings of Christ's return. Little wonder the Lord compared today's generation to the days of Noah.

Over twenty years ago, Dr. George Wald, scientist at Harvard University and recipient of the Nobel Peace Prize, made this incredibly prophetic statement: "I think human life is threatened as never before in the history of the planet. Not just by one peril, but by many perils that are all working together and coming to a head at about the same time. And that time lies very close to the year 2000. I am one of those scientists who finds it hard to see how the human race is to bring itself much past the year 2000."[2]

It must be stated that no one knows the exact time of Christ's return. In fact, Jesus said, "Of that day and hour no one knows, not even the angels of heaven, nor the Son, but the Father alone" (Matt: 24:36). So it is foolish to set dates, but we are assured once the "fig tree buds," that generation will not pass without witnessing the Lord's return.

The "Generation"

In the passage "this generation will not pass away until all these things take place" (Matt. 24:34), the Greek word for "generation" is "genea," meaning "age, generation, nation, or time."[3] The reference to "generation" seems to have a double meaning, referring to the age who has witnessed Israel become a nation *and* the nation of Israel itself will not pass away until it sees the coming of Christ. Firstly, Scripture is clear that the Jewish race will never perish: "Thus says the Lord, Who gives the sun for light by day, and the fixed order of the moon and the stars for light by night, Who stirs up the sea so that its waves roar; the Lord of hosts is His name: 'If this fixed order departs from before Me,' declares the Lord, 'then the offspring of Israel also shall cease from being a nation before Me forever'" (Jer. 31:35-36). Secondly, in 1998, Israel celebrates its fiftieth year as a nation, and with each passing decade, we continue to witness an acceleration of the prophetical signs as a woman travailing in childbirth. Therefore, Jesus' use of the word "generation" apparently indicated a span of time, and because the Jews *will* witness the return of Christ, it necessarily included a race of people.

How long then is a generation? There are a couple of suggestions. First, Webster defines a generation as "the average span of time between the birth of parents and that of their offspring," roughly twenty-five years. A second possibility may be around forty years. Scripture says the Israelites, who were led out of Egypt, wandered "in the wilderness forty years, until the entire generation of those who had done evil in the sight of the Lord was destroyed" (Num. 32:13).

Though the fig tree "became tender" in May of 1948, it actually budded or "put forth its leaves" in the Six-Day War in June of 1967 when the Jews captured Jerusalem, regaining control of their beloved city after nearly 2600 years. This was also a miracle of untold proportion. When we measure forty years from this significant event, it takes us up to the year 2007 as a possible time for Christ's return. As exciting as that is, the thrilling part for the believer is that we are removed at the Rapture seven years *before* the return of Christ, or possibly around the year 2000!

It must be noted there is significance to the repetitive use of numbers in Scripture. The number forty is used more than ninety times. It rained forty days and forty nights when the Lord destroyed the earth by the flood (Gen. 7:4, 12). Moses killed an Egyptian for beating a Hebrew, and then fled from Pharaoh to the land of Midian for forty years before God appeared to him in the burning bush (Ex. 2-3). After Moses led the Israelites out of Egypt, he went into the presence of God on Mount Sinai for forty days and forty nights where he wrote the Ten Commandments (Ex. 34:28). Because of their disobedience and rebellion toward God, the Israelites wandered in the wilderness forty years (Deut. 8:2). David was king of Israel for forty years (2 Sam. 5:4). His son Solomon also reigned over Israel forty years (2 Chr. 9:30). Jesus fasted in the wilderness forty days and forty nights before He began His three-year ministry (Matt. 4:2). And after His crucifixion and resurrection, He remained on the earth forty days before He ascended into a cloud to the Father (Acts 1:3, 9). So we see throughout Scripture a pattern regarding the number forty, and as such, the importance of the number cannot be overlooked.

Other theories have been proposed which also place

the Rapture around the year 2000. The apostle Peter wrote, "Do not let this one fact escape your notice, beloved, that with the Lord one day is as a thousand years, and a thousand years as one day" (2 Pet. 3:8). The number seven in the Bible represents completion. From Adam to Abraham was 2,000 years, from Abraham to Christ was 2,000 years, and from Christ to the present has been nearly 2,000 years. After Jesus returns, He will then reign on the earth for a thousand years. These figures total 7,000 years, and may possibly represent the perfect and complete number for humankind's existence.

Again, using the same reference of "a day is as a thousand years," in the fifth chapter of Hosea, the prophet records God's words of rebuke toward Israel for their apostasy. He concluded His rebuke with these words "I will go away and return to My place until they acknowledge their guilt and seek My face; in their affliction they will earnestly seek Me" (Hos. 5:15). Israel responded to God's rebuke by saying, "He will revive us after *two* days; He will raise us up on the *third* day that we may live before Him" (Hos. 6:2, italics mine). Since Jesus returned to His place with the Father nearly 2,000 years ago, possibly representing the two days in this passage, most of the Jews have yet to acknowledge their guilt of apostasy. While they have experienced a steady flow of persecution, the Jews will suffer tremendous affliction during the Tribulation, causing them to seek God's face, just as the passage warns. Their restoration will finally occur at the Second Coming of Christ, where afterwards they will "live before Him" during His millennial reign, or possibly as the Scripture states, "the third day." Could the new Millennium be the *third* day?

Again, no one knows the exact time, but Israel is the key to unlocking prophecy, and nearly everything regarding the end times directly revolves around her, "the apple of God's eye" (Zech. 2:8). Of course, when Jesus answered the disciples' questions on the Mount of Olives, He knew His return would be delayed for thousands of years, but He graciously gave the signs so this generation living in the apostasy of the last days would recognize them and know He is near, thereby "looking for the blessed hope and the appearing of the glory of our great God and Savior, Christ Jesus" (Titus 2:13).

Jesus listed a number of signs to be watchful for. He warned of the rise of false Christs and false prophets, wars and rumors of wars, plagues and famines, earthquakes, as well as terrors and great signs from heaven. Keep in mind, it is the frequency and intensity with which these signs are occurring which herald the imminency of Christ's return. "These things are merely the beginning of birth pains. Even so you too, when you see all these things, recognize that He is near, right at the door" (Matt. 24:8, 33).

False Christs and False Prophets

> *For many will come in My name, saying, 'I am the Christ,' and will mislead many. And many false prophets will arise, and will mislead many.*
>
> Matthew 24:5, 11

False Christs and false prophets have been around since the beginning of recorded history. Moses warned of them, as did Jeremiah, Ezekiel, the apostle Paul, Peter, and a number of others. In fact, at the time of Christ's birth in Bethlehem, a false Christ named Judas, of all things, arose in Galilee and deceived many into following him (Acts 5:37). Today, as the day draws nearer to Jesus' return, we have seen a proliferation of individuals claiming Messianic authority. False Christs and false prophets have become commonplace newsmakers. As society has increasingly separated from God and His Word, people have steadily become easier targets for deception. It is their unfamiliarity with the Scriptures that is the catalyst to accepting one's claims of Messianic authority. Scripture says, "See to it that no one takes you captive through philosophy and empty deception, according to the tradition of men, according to the elementary principles of the world, rather than according to Christ" (Col. 2:8). The rise in false Christs and false prophets is the direct result of a world which has abandoned Truth. In the last 100 years, a steady flow of deceivers have surfaced.

Near the turn of the 20th century, Baha'u'llah, also known as "God's Messenger" and the "Divine Teacher," founded the Baha'i religion, which has a current worldwide following of five million people. Among his many claims, he declared himself to be "the One promised by all religions."

In the '30s, George Baker, also known as Father Major Jealous Divine, founded the worldwide Universal Peace Mission Movement. He rose in Messianic popularity after a judge, who sentenced him to a year in jail and assessed him a $500 fine for disturbing the peace, suddenly died. Divine supposedly willed the judge's death because he interfered with his program, and as a result, Father Divine was placed in the spotlight as one possessing the power of God.

But in the past thirty years alone, we have seen a marked increase in this type of deception. As far back as the '70s, those claiming to be the Messiah include Guruji, Charles Manson, India's Maharaj Ji, Korea's Rev. Sun Myung Moon, who is still active in the '90s and founder of the Unification Church, the Children of God leader Moses David Berg, and Lord Maitreya of the New Age Avitars. Perhaps the most notorious of false Christs was the People's Temple Leader, the Rev. Jim Jones, who regarded himself as the "reincarnation of Jesus Christ." Jones even made this chilling statement: "I am peace. I am justice. I am equality. *I am God*." Tragically, in November of 1978, Jones persuaded over 900 of his devoted followers to take their own lives in a mass suicide. Those who refused to drink the cyanide-laced punch were shot to death, including Jim Jones, who was found dead with a gunshot wound to his forehead.

The '80s saw the rise of Transcendental Meditation leader "His Holiness" Maharishi Mahesh Yogi, whose New Age approach to inner peace has amassed a worldwide following of four million people. There was the late Bhagwan Shree Rajneesh, a guru from India who amassed a following of some 375,000 people worldwide. He chose the name "Bhagwan" because it meant "the embodiment of God."

The '90s saw the rise of David Koresh, leader of the Branch Davidians in Waco, Texas, referred to by some as the "Latter-Day Lamb." Gabriel of Sedona appeared on NBC's Dateline, claiming to be Jesus Christ Himself. Marshall Applewhite also claimed Messianic authority. Known as "Do," the leader of the Heaven's Gate cult, he and 38 of his followers left their "containers" by committing suicide in March of 1997. They had the misguided hope of catching a spaceship on to heaven which they believed was following behind the Hale-Bopp Comet.

Indeed, Scripture warns in the last days "evil men and imposters will proceed from bad to worse, deceiving and being deceived" (2 Tim. 3:13). We can expect false Christs and false prophets to continue until the ultimate deceivers emerge, the Antichrist and his accomplice, the False Prophet.

Wars and Rumors of Wars

> *And you will be hearing of wars and rumors of wars; see that you are not frightened, for those things must take place, but that is not yet the end. For nation will rise against nation, and kingdom against kingdom....*
>
> Matthew 24:6-7

Wars

It seems peace must be sitting under the pot of gold at the end of the rainbow. We are always pursuing it, but can never find it. Thomas a Kempis once said, "All men desire peace, but few desire those things that make for peace." Indeed, wars and conflict have raged throughout recorded history, but they have usually concentrated in a single area at a time, that is, until the 20th century.

In the past thirty years alone, more than sixty conflicts have erupted, occurring simultaneously in various parts of the world. In fact, the constant turmoil drew the attention of ABC Morning News which confirmed there has been "continual warfare somewhere on the planet since 1945."[4]

Incredibly, the 20th century has seen more than 200 major conflicts worldwide, including the Russo-Japanese War (1904-05); the Balkan wars (1912-13); World War I, (1914-18); the Spanish Civil War (1937-39); World War II (1939-

45); the Colombian Civil War (1948-53); the Korean War (1950-53); the Vietnam War (1963-73); the Lebanese Civil War (1973-82); the Angolan Civil War (1975-1991); the Iran-Iraq War (1980-88); the Afghanistan Civil War (1979-89); the Falklands War (1982); the Gulf War (1991), and the Bosnian conflict (1991-95).[5] Though not longlasting, two highly notable wars in Israel would include the Six-Day War in June of 1967, followed by the Yom Kippur War in October of 1973.

Today, there are a number of ongoing conflicts worldwide. These include the Georgian Military Revolt; the intervention in Lesotho by South Africa and Botswana; the Tutsi Congo Revolt; the Saudi-Yemen Border Conflict; the Yemeni Tribal Uprising; the Guinea-Bissau Civil War; the Burmese Civil War; the Second Eritrea-Ethiopia War; the Rwandan Civil War; the Burundi Civil War; the Algerian Civil War; the Kashmir War and Indo-Pakistan Border Conflict; the Indonesian Aceh Rebellion; the Kurdish Rebellion in Turkey; the Sri Lanka Civil War; the Sierra Leone Civil War; the Northern Ireland Conflict; and the crisis in Kosovo.[6]

All of these wars and conflicts combined have claimed the lives of more than 70 million people, making the 20th century the bloodiest era in human history.

For thousands of years, battles have been fought with basic weaponry, swords and spears, bows and arrows. In the case of David and Goliath, a slingshot and the power of God brought down the giant Philistine (1 Sam. 17:45-49). Likewise, the Spirit of the living God descended on Samson, enabling him to kill a thousand men simply with the jawbone of a donkey (Judg. 15:14-16). But the 20th century alone has seen the development of conventional, nuclear, biologic, and chemical warfare. Their development corresponds with

Daniel's prophecy that "knowledge will increase" at the end of time (Dan. 12:4).

Ironically, nuclear weapons were introduced just over fifty years ago as a means of *securing* peace. After witnessing detonation of the world's first atomic bomb on July 16, 1945, its inventor and physicist J. Robert Oppenheimer stated, "I have become Death, the destroyer of worlds."[7] Less than a month later, the people of Hiroshima and Nagasaki, Japan, were the target of his prophetic words. No wonder Solomon wrote, "In much wisdom there is much grief, and increasing knowledge results in increasing pain" (Eccl. 1:18). And so today, in an effort to secure peace, mankind has compiled enough nuclear weapons to blow the earth all the way to Pluto. But nuclear weapons do incalculable destruction to the earth and its atmosphere, so it was incumbent upon physicists to develop more streamlined weapons of mass destruction. Today, we secure the peace with chemical and biological weapons.

Chemical agents include vesicants which burn or blister the skin of its victims, lung-damaging agents which choke, and blood agents which also cause choking. All of these chemical agents can be dispersed by either artillery shells, mortar shells, rockets, land mines, missiles, aircraft spray, or aircraft bombs.[8] Nerve agents, such as Tabun and Sarin, are among the deadliest of chemical agents. On March 20, 1995, during the morning rush hour, members of the cult Aum Shinri Kyo, or the Supreme Truth, released the nerve agent Sarin into a Tokyo subway system, killing 12 people and injuring thousands.

Biological warfare would include weapons containing viruses, bacteria, or biological toxins. The viruses may include Ebola, the Hanta Virus, or Venezuelan Equine Encephalitis, causing, respectively, hemorrhagic fever, respiratory distress, and swelling of the brain. Bacterial agents may include Vibrio cholera, causing gastroenteritis which results in up to one liter of fluid loss per hour; Yersinia pestis, causing lung fever and swollen lymph nodes; and Bacillus anthracis, the causative agent of anthrax, a disease which causes boils on the skin and lesions on the lungs. Biological toxins are extremely potent and include botulinum toxin and Clostridium perfringens. Botulinum toxin produces respiratory paralysis, causing its victims to suffocate. An estimated one gram of botulinum can kill up to ten million people. Clostridium perfringens cause necrotism, or death of the flesh.[9]

As scary as all this sounds, the fact is, these weapons will definitely be used someday during the Tribulation. Scripture warns, "...their flesh will rot while they stand on their feet, and their eyes will rot in their sockets, and their tongue will rot in their mouth" (Zech. 14:12). Scripture also warns "loathsome and malignant sores" (Rev. 16:2) will form on men's skin, a clear indication of radioactivity, or even possibly that of chemical and biological activity.

Countries currently possessing biological and chemical weapons include China, Taiwan, North Korea, Syria, Egypt, Iran, Iraq, Cuba, Israel, the former Soviet States, Japan, and the United States.[10]

Rumors of Wars

The Cuban Missile Crisis is perhaps the most notable rumor of war during this 20th century. Less than twenty years after detonation of the first nuclear warhead, two of the world's superpowers, the United States and the former Soviet Republic, were locked in a show of force for two weeks in October of 1962. Shortly afterward, Anatoly Gribkov, Soviet Republic and Army Chief of Operations, stated, "Nuclear catastrophe was hanging by a thread...and we weren't counting days or hours, but minutes."

More recently, in February of 1998, another rumor of war occurred as the United States postured against Iraqi leader Saddam Hussein for failing to allow United Nations weapons inspectors to search suspected facilities for the storage of chemical and biological weapons. Again, a standoff ensued between the nations, heightened by Russian President Boris Yeltsin's threat to intervene on Iraq's behalf if the U.S. acted on its threats. Finally, United Nations Secretary-General Kofi Annan stepped up and initiated discussions with Saddam Hussein, who then relented at the eleventh hour.

In May of 1998, yet another nuclear crisis arose. Rumors of war were flying in South Asia as a result of India's underground detonation of five sub-kiloton nuclear warheads. Understandably feeling threatened, neighboring Pakistan followed suit with the underground detonation of five of their own nuclear warheads. India and Pakistan have been longstanding rivals, having engaged in two conflicts since 1947. Today, the neighboring countries are engaged in heated discussions regarding drug trafficking and the rise of alleged Pakistani state-sponsored terrorists settling into the Indian regions of Jammu and Kashmir. If the matter is not resolved, the situation could potentially escalate into a serious conflict.

As history is often destined to repeat itself, in November of 1998, Saddam Hussein once again refused to allow inspectors from UNSCOM, the United Nations Special Commission, to search suspected facilities for the storage of chemical and biological weapons used during the Iran-Iraq War in the 1980's. This time, Iraqis vowed not to back down to threats of air strikes from the United States, and other Arab leaders urged Saddam Hussein to relent. In his refusal, the necessary troops and machinery were deployed to the region, and once again, Hussein relented at the eleventh hour. Albert Einstein once said, "Every kind of peaceful cooperation among men is primarily based on mutual trust." The United States' victory in the standoff seems a hollow one, as Saddam Hussein continually demonstrates his inability to be trusted.

At the close of World War II, General Douglas MacArthur made this chilling statement: "Men since the beginning of time have sought peace...military alliances, balances of power, leagues of nations all in turn failed, leaving the only path to be by way of the crucible of war. We have had our last chance. If we do not now devise some greater and more equitable system, Armageddon will be at our door."[11]

Unfortunately, wars and rumors of wars will continue, and there will be no peace on earth until Jesus returns at the battle of Armageddon and thereafter sets up His righteous millennial kingdom. In the meantime, the peace men search for can only be found in Jesus Christ. In fact, He said, "In Me you may have peace. In the world you have tribulation, but take courage; I have overcome the world" (John 16:33).

Finally, in the Valley of Megiddo in Israel, all the nations of the world will gather for the battle of Armageddon (Rev. 16:14, 16). However, it will not be the last conflict for mankind. Scripture reveals a final war at the conclusion of the Millennium (Rev. 20:7-9).

Plagues and Famines

> *There will be...in various places plagues and famines....*
>
> Luke 21:11

Plagues

Plagues and famines have been around since the days of the Israelites. But today, we are not only witnessing the return of diseases once considered eradicated, we are seeing new strains of infectious diseases that make the plagues of Egypt look like ants at a picnic. In fact, infectious diseases are the leading cause of death worldwide and were the third cause of death in the United States in 1992.[12] As the day draws near for the return of Christ, we are seeing the steady increase of plagues, just as Jesus predicted.

In 1979, the first case of AIDS, Acquired Immune Deficiency Syndrome, was reported. By the end of 1997, a staggering 11.7 million people have died worldwide from the disease, and more than 30.6 million people are now living with AIDS or HIV, the human immunodeficiency virus which causes AIDS. What's more, current figures show an estimated 16,000 people a day are contracting the deadly virus[13] for which there is still no cure. This disease is no longer considered an epidemic, but a pandemic.

Cholera, malaria, and tuberculosis were once controlled, but have made a strong comeback in recent years. In January of 1991, an epidemic of cholera broke out in South

America and quickly spread to other countries, claiming thousands of lives. Without treatment, severe cases of cholera can result in death within hours.[14] Malaria, once the leading cause of death around the world, was considered eradicated by the 1960's. Today, malaria infects more than 270 million people worldwide, killing more than two million each year.[15] In the early '90s, an outbreak of malaria was reported in New Jersey, New York, and Texas.[16] Tuberculosis is on the decrease in the United States, but in March of 1998, the World Health Organization announced that tuberculosis has again become a major global problem, with one billion people likely to become infected and 70 million expected to die within the next twenty years.[17]

Dengue and dengue hemorrhagic fever has re-emerged throughout the world, with more than 100 million cases of dengue and hundreds of thousands of dengue hemorrhagic fever reported annually.[18] It is a mosquito-borne viral disease comparable to malaria. After a lengthy absence, dengue fever has also resurfaced in the United States.

We have further seen the emergence of the Ebola virus, first detected in Africa in 1976; the foodborne bacteria E. coli, first traced to hamburger meat in 1982; the Hanta Virus, transmitted by diseased rats, which first appeared in the "Four Corners" region of the United States in May of 1993; an outbreak of Monkeypox in Congo beginning in February of 1996; and a terrifying strain of flesh-eating bacteria which surfaced in the mid-90's. In April of 1997, the World Health Organization announced "at least thirty new infectious diseases, with no known treatment, cure, or vaccine, have emerged in the past twenty years." This is just as the Lord said it would be prior to His return to earth.

Famines

In the 20th century, widespread famine began in the 1970's as a result of the population explosion. Experts have calculated that it took from the *beginning of time* to 1850 A.D., for the world population to reach one billion. But from 1850 to 1930, the population grew exponentially, reaching its second billion. From 1930 to 1960, just thirty short years, we reached our third billion. From 1960 to 1975, in only fifteen years, the world population grew to four billion.[19]

And now approaching the year 2000, we have nearly six billion people on the planet. Unfortunately, most countries are not able to produce the food needed to feed their own citizens and rely heavily on other nations to supply their food. But changing global weather patterns, causing drought, severe flooding, and a number of other environmental factors, have led to disastrous crop failures and an overall shortage of food production, making it exceedingly difficult to feed an ever-growing world population. In fact, in the United States, the world's breadbasket, food reserves of grain and corn are at their lowest levels in sixteen years, while wheat reserves are at its lowest level in nearly fifty years, yet we continually reach into our supply to meet the needs of the starving in other countries. The global situation is critical.

Famine can also be a man-made peril, the direct result of war. Raging conflicts create an inability to distribute food, and millions face starvation. Since the '70s, Asia and Africa have continually been plagued by famine due to drought and warring factions. Hundreds of thousands of people died of starvation in Cambodia in the late '70s. In the mid-'80s, nearly a million people starved to death in Ethiopia. In the early '90s, famine killed hundreds of thousands in Somalia.

Today, in 1998, the African continent remains in desperate need of food relief. In Ethiopia, 800,000 people are starving due to drought and a poor harvest. The war-torn Sudanese nation is experiencing famine. According to the United Nations World Food Program, 2.6 million people are currently at risk of starvation, while 1.5 million have already died.[20]

In the Philippines, severe drought has caused a shortage of food production, leaving 300,000 in need of food. North Korea is suffering a critical famine as well. To date, an estimated three million people have died of starvation,[21] and nearly five million are malnourished, subsisting on 600 calories a day or less. A two-million-ton shortfall in grain production due to drought and flooding, combined with Communist mismanagement, are all factors in the crisis.[22]

Drought conditions in Russia have also created a tremendous crisis. Russia is expected to harvest a scant 52 million tons of grain this year, hardly enough to sustain the country through the winter months. It is their worst crop since the 1950's. The United States has proposed a $500 million support package, to include 1.5 million tons of wheat, along with 1.5 million tons of meat, provided Moscow promises to distribute the aid fairly.[23]

As if all this were not devastating enough, there is a terrible 3½-year drought on the horizon at the commencement of the Tribulation (Rev. 11:6).

Earthquakes

> *In various places there will be...earthquakes.*
>
> Matthew 24:7

Earthquakes are one of the most frightening catastrophes known to man. They strike without warning, destroying lives and communities in a matter of minutes. These, too, are nothing new to this generation. In fact, major earthquakes have been recorded throughout history, their story carved on everything from cave walls to pyramids. Scripture itself records four earthquakes, including the severe quake which occurred at the resurrection of Jesus (Matt. 28:2). But some would have us to believe the number of earthquakes we are experiencing today is unchanged from the beginning of time; the only difference being advanced seismic technology to better monitor the earth's movement. Certainly geologists can more accurately track earthquakes today, but even *since* the development of this technology, there has been an enormous increase in seismic activity.

The World Almanac contains a listing of major earthquakes, measuring 5.5 or greater on the Richter scale, that have occurred worldwide since 526 A.D. From that year to 856 A.D., over a 330-year period, there were only two major earthquakes. The next major earthquake occurred 200 years later, in 1057 A.D. From that time to 1900 A.D., spanning nearly 850 years, there were a total of 21 major earthquakes, with ten- to thirty-year gaps in between. Seismic activity was relatively quiet.[24]

The 20th century changed all that. From 1900 to 1950, there were *21* major earthquakes recorded, averaging two to four years apart. Incredibly, from 1950 to 1997, there have been an astounding *93* major earthquakes. Those occurring from 1950 to 1960 were about three years apart; from 1960 to 1970, two years; from 1970 to 1980, one year; from 1980 to 1990, six months to a year; with the decade of the '90s showing the most startling figures yet. From 1990 to 1995, there were as many as four major earthquakes a *year*. And in one year's time alone, from July 1996 to July 1997, there were *26* major earthquakes worldwide,[25] and already 24 within the first four months of 1998![26]

In 1973, the U.S. Geological Survey, a branch of the Department of the Interior, established the National Earthquake Information Center. The NEIC provides rapid reports of seismic activity to scientists and governmental agencies throughout the world, as well as the general public. It has an extensive seismic database, with more than 3,000 national and international reporting networks stationed in some 80 countries, making it *the* premier information center in the United States for earthquake data retrieval. According to the NEIC, there are "many millions" of earthquakes occurring every year measuring 4.5 or less on the Richter scale.[27]

Though the world has never experienced shaking to the degree it will soon, some of the most devastating earthquakes have certainly left their indelible marks. On Good Friday, March 27, 1964, at 5:36 P.M., the earth shook for nearly four minutes beneath Anchorage, Alaska, in what is the longest recorded earthquake in U.S. history. Measuring an astonishing 8.6 on the Richter scale, this geologic catastrophe cut a 500-mile path of destruction, creating fissures in the earth as wide as thirty feet. The quake released energy equivalent to 12,000 Hiroshima-type atomic bombs, or 240 million tons of TNT. It heaved 100,000 square miles of the earth's surface upward, resulting in the "greatest area of vertical displacement ever measured in earthquake history."[28] It sent shock waves thousands of miles. Incredibly, the ground beneath Houston, Texas, momentarily raised four inches from the radiating waves.[29]

When the earth finally stopped shaking, 131 lives were lost, many of whom were never found, and 25,000 square miles of land had been moved from its place. Anchorage was moved six feet toward the sea, while neighboring Valdez moved 33 feet and Seward, 47. The force of the quake caused the entire planet to shake for two more weeks, though the aftershocks around Anchorage were felt for eighteen months, as the ground continued to quake more than 10,000 times.[30]

As powerful as the Alaskan earthquake was, it will pale in comparison to the reeling of the earth at the end of the Tribulation. At that time, there will be "a great earthquake, such as there has not been since man came to be upon the earth, so great an earthquake, and so mighty (that) every island fled away, and the mountains were not found" (Rev. 16:18, 20).

Terrors and Great Signs in the Heavens

> *There will be...in various places...terrors and great signs from heaven.*
>
> Luke 21:11

Three different heavens may be seen in Scripture. The first heaven is the air we breathe, the space around us and above us where birds fly and airplanes soar. The second is the celestial heaven or the universe with its stars, planets, and galaxies. The third heaven is the home of God.

The Weather

One could scarcely imagine the intense changing weather patterns and subsequent calamities that have befallen this decade. Floods, hurricanes, typhoons, droughts abound. Meteorologists have placed the blame on El Nino, a warm weather pattern that builds in the Pacific Ocean over a period of months. What causes it is still a mystery, but scientists could possibly find a clue in the name. Peruvian fishermen gave the name "El Nino" to a weather system that appeared every year around Christmas. "El Nino" refers to "the Christ child," and all this unusual weather is a sign from Him to the world that He is near, "right at the door."

The weather has been erratic for the past thirty years, but the '90s have been unprecedented. In the last eight years, there have been 12 occasions of destructive tornadoes sweeping the U.S., five major cyclones hitting Asia; another five typhoons hitting Asia and the Philippines; eleven tropical storms and a monsoon hitting the Caribbeans, the U.S., and Mexico; four Siberian-type blizzards and an ice storm hitting the U.S., with seven worldwide volcanic eruptions and 19 states in the U.S. experiencing record-breaking temperatures since 1980, including Arizona's blistering 128 degrees set on June 29, 1994.[31] And in a year's time, from 1996 to 1997, there were "as many as 8,000 national disasters" in the U.S.[32]

Since 1995, there have been 28 hurricanes, including Hurricane Bonnie in August of 1998 which did over $1 billion in damage. And in September of 1998, for the first time in over a century, since 1892, four hurricanes, namely, Karl, Georges, Ivan, and Jeanne, occurred simultaneously in the Atlantic Ocean. According to meteorologist Michele Huber at the National Hurricane Center in Miami, "This is definitely something beyond the ordinary."[33]

In the last week of October 1998, Hurricane Mitch slammed into Central America with winds over 180 miles an hour, killing more than 10,000 people and making it one of the deadliest Atlantic storms on record. The hurricane dumped as much as two feet of rain a day, causing thousands to be killed in mudslides alone. And to compound matters, the Cerro Negro volcano in Nicaragua erupted, spewing lava, hot gas, and flaming rocks down on the devastated region.[34]

And what of all the flooding? From 1228 A.D. to 1900, over nearly 675 years, there were only five major floods or tidal waves recorded. In less than 100 years, since the beginning of the 20th century, there have been 90 major floods worldwide, 56 of them occurring since 1970.[35]

A recent article in Life Magazine stated, "Since the beginning of 1997, more than 16,000 have been killed worldwide by the weather and nearly $50 billion in damage has been done. In the U.S., the figures are 456 dead and $13 billion lost. While there have been cataclysms of greater immensity and intensity in our century, the distribution, variety and frequency of the recent rotten weather has been extraordinary."[36]

In July of 1998, meteorologists officially declared the El Nino weather pattern over, but as we have already seen, more surprises await. Scripture warns, "There will be signs in sun and moon and stars, and upon the earth dismay among the nations, in perplexity at the roaring of the sea, and the waves, men fainting from fear and the expectation of the things which are coming upon the whole world; for the powers of the heavens will be shaken" (Luke 21:25-26).

Unexplained Phenomena

"In the beginning God created the heavens and the earth" (Gen. 1:1). "For by Him *all* things were created, both in the heavens and on earth, visible and invisible, whether thrones or dominions or rulers or authorities—*all* things have been created by Him and for Him" (Col. 1:16, emphasis mine).

That means everything—dinosaurs, Bigfoot, Sasquatch, Yetti, the Boggy Creek Monster, the Lochness Monster, the Bermuda Triangle, Atlantis, poltergeists, UFOs, and whatever else there may be out there. Try as we might, there are some things we are just not going to know about. But God knows everything. He is in control of all things, and nothing happens that He does not allow.

Because Jesus is about to return, the god of this world, Satan, and all his minions are working overtime to deceive people into believing anything but the truth. As believers, we know "truth is in Jesus" (Eph. 4:21), and no matter what we see with our eyes, if it conflicts with the Scriptures, it is a lie from the devil, sent to confuse and distort the truth. The apostle Paul warned of this. "The Spirit explicitly says that in later times some will fall away from the faith, paying attention to deceitful spirits and doctrines of demons" (1 Tim. 4:1).

Over the past thirty years, we have seen an explosion of unexplained phenomena. There have been millions of UFO sightings around the world, with thousands of people claiming alien abduction. Of course, Hollywood has pounced on all the fascination with the unknown by bombarding us with television shows like Star Trek; X-Files; Millennium; Sightings; Alien Nation; Earth: Final Conflict; Fox's Alien Autopsy; Third Rock from the Sun; Roswell: The UFO Cover-Up; as well as movies like Independence Day; ET; Enemy Mine; Star Trek: The Movie; Star Wars; Close Encounters of the Third Kind; Men in Black; 2001: A Space Odyssey; Contact, and the list goes on and on.

It is not a coincidence that we are seeing all this heightened alien and UFO activity at this crucial time before Jesus returns. It is essential to the end-time scenario so that when the Rapture happens, there can be a satisfactory explanation for the hundreds of millions of persons who have disappeared. Let us consider some of this groundwork.

In March of 1997, in a suburb outside of San Diego, California, 39 members of the Heaven's Gate cult took their own lives in an effort to get on board what they believed was a spaceship bound for heaven following behind the Hale-Bopp Comet. With all its haunting pictures and details, this tragedy got enormous media attention and actually set the stage for the eventual explanation of the Rapture.

Then, in December of 1997, members of the cult God's Salvation Church began gathering in Garland, Texas, to await God's arrival in a spaceship on March 31 of 1998. He didn't show.

In January of 1998, in Madrid, Spain, a thirty-member sect, linked with the Solar Temple cult, attempted to commit suicide, also believing they would be carried away by a spaceship from the summit of Tenerife's Teide volcano. Fortunately, the police intervened as cult members were staging their "last supper" at a private home. In 1994, however, 74 members of the Solar Temple cult did commit suicide.

Finally, in March of 1998, again in Garland, Texas, a 150-member Taiwanese sect, led by Hon-Ming Chen, claimed that God would appear just after midnight on Channel 18, of any United States television set, to announce His plans for the following week. Chen and his followers believed God was going to descend to earth to take hundreds of millions of people to another planet by, what else, flying saucers in order to save us from a nuclear holocaust in 1999.

Because the Rapture is so close, all these events are acts of demonic deception, clearly orchestrated in order to provide an acceptable answer for the whereabouts of millions of missing people. The proliferation of UFO sightings and the unexplained phenomena are all part of an agenda God is permitting for the end times. Scripture says, "I will grant wonders in the sky above, and signs on the earth beneath" (Acts 2:19).

Another plausible explanation for the disappearance of millions may be attributed to the cosmos. On August 27, 1998, the most powerful energy burst ever detected from beyond the solar system struck the earth over the Pacific Ocean. For five minutes, "It was as if night was briefly turned into day in the ionosphere," states Umran Inan of Stanford University. A neutron star, known as a magnetar, burst about 20,000 light-years away in the Earth's galaxy, the Milky Way. The star's magnetic field is billions of times stronger than anything on earth and 100 times stronger than any previously discovered in the universe. It did not come closer than thirty miles from the earth's surface, but researchers have identified this event as the first occasion a significant change has occurred in the earth's environment due to energy released from a distant star. According to Robert Duncan of the University of Texas, "A magnet this strong could erase the magnetic strip on the credit cards in your wallet or pull the keys out of your pocket from a distance halfway to the moon."[37] Perhaps some will suggest it could even pull people off the planet.

Consider the Comet Shoemaker-Levy 9 which in July 1994 collided with the planet Jupiter, releasing more energy into Jupiter's atmosphere than all of the world's nuclear arsenal combined. The collision of a large comet with a planet is considered an extraordinary, millennial event.[38]

Further, on November 17, 1998, satellite companies the world over braced themselves for the most intense Leonid meteor storm in over thirty years as the earth passed through the debris of the Temple-Tuttle Comet. The small, dust-like particles of the comet entered the earth's atmosphere at about 155,000 miles an hour and then burned up, but they nonetheless posed a threat of striking any one of the 600 satellites orbiting the earth which broadcast television shows and transmit pagers and cell phones.[39]

No doubt there has been heightened anxiety over comets and asteroids hitting the earth, with scientists confirming the likelihood of such an occurrence someday. Movies like

Deep Impact, Asteroid, and Armageddon have also contributed to the fear of being obliterated from space.

The truth of the matter is, no comets or asteroids are likely to hit the earth, but within the next five-year period, from 1998 to 2003, more than eighty comets are expected to pass by. With the Rapture so close, it will seem a plausible explanation to suggest the missing are in spaceships following behind one or any number of these comets. Again, nothing happens that God does not permit, and with strange or once-in-a-lifetime event we seem to keep experiencing in our lifetime, will ultimately play a part in the end-time agenda as an explanation for the Rapture. All the UFO activity, as well as the neutron stars and comets, are part of the "wonders in the sky" surrounding the last days.

And what of the "signs on the earth beneath"? Since 1973, there have been more than 9,000 documented cases of crop circle formations on the earth, 90% of which have been in England. Colin Andrews, founder and president of Circles Phenomenon Research International, recently interviewed Col. Philip J. Corso, (Ret.), who stated, "Crop circles are known to be real by the U.S. government."[40] Andrews became interested in the phenomenon in 1983 after viewing a field containing five circles which were aligned in the shape of a cross.

When the circles first appeared, the magnitude of the situation was so inexplicable, that to avert a public panic, the British government and the CIA fabricated the story of two elderly men named Doug and Dave, who had nothing better to do in the wee hours of the morning than to pull off an incredible hoax. It was later discovered that the two men were paid to perpetuate the story.

In fact, it is not humanly possible to fabricate a perfect crop circle formation. Crop circles are of extremely complex Euclidian geometry. After their formation, there is an increase in infra red output in and around the new formation. There is an altered magnetic structure, which causes a failure in compasses to point north, the failure of watches and cameras to operate, as well as equipment failure on aircraft flying over the formation. The air within the formation is also disturbed, causing Geiger counters to record higher levels of radiation and voltameters to read higher and lower levels of electricity. Animals are extremely agitated hours before a formation appears, and car batteries in entire villages have failed to operate the morning after a formation is found.[41]

What's more, the unexplained phenomenon has driven farmers, the military, scientists, and untold numbers of enthusiasts into the fields to catch a glimpse of whatever is causing these geometrical figures. Yet even with all the top surveillance equipment, including high-tech laser devices, crop circles just "appear" out of nowhere.[42]

Again, all this unexplained phenomena is a master work of deception, orchestrated by "deceitful spirits" (1 Tim. 4:1) at this critical time in order to convince the masses of the existence of extraterrestrial life. Make no mistake, *Christians* are the only aliens in this land, and when Jesus comes to take us to heaven, we are not going in spaceships.

The Days of Lot

And just as it happened in the days of Noah, so it shall be also in the days of the Son of Man: they were eating, they were drinking, they were marrying, they were being given in marriage...it was the same as happened in the days of Lot.

Luke 17:26-28

Jesus not only compared the generation who would witness His return to that of Noah's days, but He also compared it to the days of Lot. Today, we are witnessing the fulfillment of these prophetic words. Since the early 1970's, homosexual men and women have been petitioning the courts and state legislators to pass laws recognizing same-sex unions. While this remains a hotbed of controversy in the United States, an increasing number of countries are currently recognizing same-sex unions.

Not surprisingly, in 1989, Denmark became the first country to legalize gay marriages, and today there are more than 4,000 recorded unions. In 1993, Norway became the second country to legalize gay marriages, followed by Sweden and Hungary in 1995. Also in 1995, six cities in Spain began recognizing same-sex unions, including Barcelona, as well as 90 Dutch towns in the Netherlands. Finland, Slovenia, Iceland, and the Czech Republic are expected to follow suit.

As of the date of this writing, there are no states legally recognizing gay marriages in the United States, but it is likely to change soon. In Hawaii, a landmark case is currently before the state legislature involving three same-sex couples requesting marriage licenses. It is likely the courts will rule in favor of the couples. Cities and states across the nation await the ruling in this case to determine whether they will grant marriage licenses to same-sex couples.

Meanwhile, in San Francisco, Mayor Willie Brown and several city officials attended a civic wedding ceremony uniting fifty same-sex couples in March of 1998. Two years prior, 163 same-sex couples exchanged vows in a domestic partners ceremony. Under the domestic partners ordinance adopted by San Francisco in the early '90s, same-sex couples can register their committed unions with the City. Since then, more than 3,000 couples have registered. To date, however, the state of California has not recognized any of these unions as legal.

The Condition of the Human Race

In the last days, difficult times will come. For men will be lovers of self, lovers of money, boastful, arrogant, revilers, disobedient to parents, ungrateful, unholy, unloving, irreconcilable, malicious gossips, without self-control, brutal, haters of good, treacherous, reckless, conceited, lovers of pleasure rather than lovers of God; holding to a form of godliness, although they have denied its power.

2 Timothy 3:1-5

In 1990, authors Peter Kim and James Patterson conducted the largest national survey of private morals ever undertaken in any nation. The survey was done in order to assess the level of personal ethics, values, and beliefs in America. In every region of the United States, respondents agreed to answer over 1,800 questions truthfully, with the guarantee of total anonymity. The shocking results were published in their book, *The Day America Told the Truth,* (Prentice Hall Press, 1991).

Of those responding, 93% said *they* determine their *own* moral values; 84% said they would violate the established rules of their religion; and 81% said they had violated a law because they felt it was wrong in their own view.[43] It was determined that 77% of the respondents failed to see the point in observing the Sabbath; 74% would steal from someone if they thought the item would not be missed; 64% would lie about a specific matter if it does not cause any harm, while 91% lie regularly; 56% said they would drink and drive; 53% said they would commit adultery; and 41% acknowledged recreational drug use.[44]

When Americans were questioned what they would do for $10 million, two-thirds responded they would: abandon their entire family (25%); abandon their church (25%); become prostitutes for a week or more (23%); give up their American citizenship (16%); leave their spouses (16%); withhold testimony and let a murderer go free (10%); kill a stranger (7%); change their race (6%); have a sex-change operation (4%); and put their children up for adoption (3%).[45]

When it came to matters of spirituality, only ten percent believed in all of the Ten Commandments, and 40% believed in five or less. Six out of seven people felt it was okay not to believe in God. Yet 46% felt they were going to heaven and only four percent felt they were going to hell.[46] I wonder where the other 50% think they are going.

Finally, by the end of 1996, the United States, a nation once founded on Christian principles, had nearly 1.2 million people locked up in federal and state penitentiaries for crime, more than 3,000 of whom are awaiting the death penalty.[47]

We hardly need statistics to confirm the endless depth of human depravity. One need only watch daytime talk shows and the evening news. The condition of the human race is precisely as the apostle Paul said it would be prior to the Lord's return.

Travel and Technology

> At the end of time, many will go back and forth, and knowledge will increase.
>
> Daniel 12:4

Travel

In this passage, the Hebrew word "shuwt" is used, meaning "to lash, i.e., the sea with oars, to row; by implication, to travel."[48] Man has traveled by boat for thousands of years. In fact, we know nearly 800 years before Christ's incarnation that Jonah "found a ship which was going to Tarshish" (Jon. 1:3). But when it came to traveling by land, man has not been quite so innovative.

For almost 6,000 years, travel across land had either been on foot or on the backs of animals. Over the years, there were some good transportational ideas, amounting to chariots in ancient times, leading up to stagecoaches and covered wagons in the 1800's. But as fast as this was compared to traveling on foot, it was still not fast enough. So beginning in the early 1800's, attention was given to developing faster forms of travel, and by the end of that century, trains had become the main source of transportation, with automobiles just beginning to emerge. There were even some fanatics who believed we could travel by air, of all things, which posed quite a challenge.

But on December 17, 1903, Orville and Wilbur Wright made a breakthrough. Near Kitty Hawk, North Carolina, the two brothers flew the first motorized plane to ever carry a human being. They each flew two flights, with the longest distance measuring 852 feet and lasting a total of 59 seconds.[49]

Today, in as little as a hundred years, modes of travel have been mastered. We cross the oceans in cruise ships weighing literally 100,000 tons and reaching as high as 14-story buildings. In Europe, commuters can cross the land in trains reaching speeds in excess of 300 miles an hour. Vehicles of every shape, size, and color enable us to get anywhere at anytime. And aviation has improved more than slightly since Orville and Wilbur's days. Jets and airbuses take us around the world in a matter of hours. Nearly 70 million people a year travel out of Chicago's O'Hare Airport, the busiest airport in the United States, while London's Heathrow Airport is the busiest internationally, with nearly 60 million worldwide travelers a year.[50]

Indeed, the 20th century has seen many traveling to and fro, just as the prophet Daniel predicted.

Technology

John the apostle wrote, "There are also many other things which Jesus did, which if they were written in detail, I suppose that even the world itself would not contain the books which were written" (John 21:25).

In the same way, it is certainly impossible for any one book to contain, let alone detail, the explosion of knowledge and technology the 20th century has seen. Whatever was invented before this century has certainly been perfected, and there is nothing of which my mind can conceive that mankind does not have at its disposal. At the end of the 19th century, someone said, "All that can be invented has been invented." And here we are at the end of the 20th century, and for the life of me, I cannot imagine what remains to be invented. We can see where things will be perfected, but what is there that man does not already have?

Medical advancement has gone through the roof. Recently, in Houston, Texas, a young boy miraculously survived a tragedy in which 99% of his body was burned. Doctors found an area of skin the size of a postage stamp on his heel that had not been burned. They removed it and sent it to a laboratory where they have already reproduced over half of the boy's skin which will eventually be grafted back onto his body.

We can even choose the sex and features of our unborn children by selecting various chromosomal DNA and injecting them into a fertilized egg to be placed into a woman's uterus. Animals have been cloned, and but for the bureaucratic red tape, it is likely the technology would already have been used on humans. In November of 1998, a chilling discovery was made in cloning technology. Scientists are now able to fuse human and animal cells together, with the possible result of creating a human-animal species. Their intent, however, is to grow organs for transplant use.

In this century, we have gone from learning to fly, to placing a man on the moon only thirty years ago, to making routine trips into outer space so astronauts can do repairs to satellites or even dock and live on space stations for months. We have vessels which can take us to the bottom of the sea where the pressure alone could flatten a man to the width of paper. At the beginning of the 20th century, it took weeks to get information around the globe, but today we witness events live on television from anyplace on the planet or send instantaneous messages all over the world via the Internet.

In 1876, Alexander Graham Bell invented the telephone. On January 25, 1915, he made the first transcontinental telephone call. From New York, he phoned Thomas A. Watson in San Francisco.[51] Today, we can talk to anyone around the world at any time of the day or night with such clarity in the connection we feel as though we are only rooms apart.

We can simulate reality by virtual reality. We can reach into an endless well of information through the World Wide Web. Computers can do absolutely anything you want them to do. In fact, they can perform a function faster than you can blink. Does anyone even ask how things work anymore?

It is impossible to adequately detail all the accomplishments of the 20th century, but suffice it to say, the knowledge explosion fulfills Daniel's words regarding the condition of the human race at the time of the end.

In summation, all of these signs have been given so that the generation which would witness them occurring *simultaneously* would know that the Lord Jesus is about to return, yes, even "right at the door."

> *Behold, I have told you in advance.*
>
> Matthew 24:25

Endnotes

1) Mark Twain, as quoted from the World's Greatest Library, in *Apocalypse Next*, William R. Goetz (Horizon Books, Camp Hill, Pennsylvania, 1996), p. 81.
2) Hal Lindsey, *The 1980's: Countdown to Armageddon* (Bantam Books, New York, 1980), p. 17.
3) Spiros Zodhiates, Th.D., ed., *Hebrew-Greek Key Study Bible, King James Version* (World Bible Publishers, 1991), Dictionary of the Greek Testament, James Strong, S.T.D., L.L.D., No. 1074, p. 20.
4) William R. Goetz, *Apocalypse Next* (Horizon Books, Camp Hill, Pennsylvania, 1996), p. 35.
5) Ibid., p. 261.
6) Lee, R. "New and Recent Conflicts of the World," http://www.historyguy.com/new_and_recent_conflicts.html (1998).
7) Rod Olsen Research Services, "Research Trials, Triumphs and Tragedies," Miller D, Miller I, Miller J, and Miller M, The Cambridge Dictionary of Scientists, (Cambridge University Press,Cambridge, UK, 1996).
8) NATO Manual FM8-285-Part I, Chapters 1-6.
9) Scott D. McCulloch, "Biological Warfare and the Implications of Biotechnology," CalPoly Institute Seminar.
10) Ibid.
11) As quoted by Hal Lindsey, *The 1980's: Countdown to Armageddon* (Bantam Books, New York, 1980), p. 24.
12) National Center for Infectious Diseases, Centers for Disease Control and Prevention, Atlanta, Georgia, May 28, 1997.
13) "Report on the Global HIV/AIDS Epidemic," UNAIDS and the World Health Or-

ganization, November 26, 1997.

14) "Cholera Prevention," National Center for Infectious Diseases, Centers for Disease Control and Prevention, Atlanta, Georgia, August 9, 1996.

15) Hal Lindsey, *Planet Earth—2000 A.D.,* (Western Front, Ltd., Palos Verdes, California, 1994), pp. 114-115.

16) Jane R. Zucker, M.D., "Changing Patterns of Autochthonous Malaria Transmission in the United States: A Review of Recent Outbreaks," Centers for Disease Control and Prevention, Atlanta, Georgia, January - March, 1996.

17) Source: MSNBC.

18) "Information on Dengue Fever and Dengue Hemorrhagic Fever," Division of Vector-Borne Infectious Diseases, National Center for Infectious Diseases, Centers for Disease Control and Prevention, March 1998.

19) *The World Almanac and Book of Facts 1998,* (K-III Reference Corporation, 1997), p. 553.

20) CNN Report, July 16, 1998.

21) Source: Reuters.

22) Source: MSNBC.

23) Source: Reuters.

24) *The World Almanac and Book of Facts 1998,* (K-III Reference Corporation, 1997), p. 269.

25) Ibid., pp. 269-270.

26) National Earthquake Information Center, U.S. Geologic Survey.

27) Fact Sheet 125-97, National Earthquake Information Center, U.S. Geologic Survey.

28) Quoted from Bruce A. Bolt, *Earthquakes* (W. H. Freeman and Company, New York, 1993), p. 11.

29) Bryce Walker, *Planet Earth—Earthquakes* (Time Life Books, Alexandria, Virginia, 1982), pp. 18-35.

30) Ibid., pp. 18-35.

31) *The World Almanac and Book of Facts 1998,* (K-III Reference Corporation, 1997), pp. 180, 268, 588-589; FEMA—Reference Library: Disaster Archives.

32) American Red Cross.

33) Lowe's Storm '98 Hurricane Central: Latest Reports; www.storm98.com.

34) Source: Reuters.

35) CNN; *The World Almanac and Book of Facts 1998,* (K-III Reference Corporation, 1997), p. 269.

36) Kenneth Miller, "Weather," *Life Magazine,* August 1998 Edition.

37) Sawyer, Kathy, *The Washington Post,* September 30, 1998, p. A01.

38) NASA, Jet Propulsion Laboratory.

39) Source: Reuters.

40) Colin Andrews, Circles Phenomenon Research International, Branford, Connecticut.

41) Colin Andrews, "The Crop Circular," Circles Phenomenon Research International, Branford, Connecticut.

42) Ibid.

43) James Patterson, Peter Kim, *The Day America Told the Truth* (Prentice Hall Press, 1991), p. 27.

44) Ibid., pp. 25-26.

45) Ibid., p. 66.

46) Ibid., pp. 200-201.

47) "Prison Population: Bureau of Justice Statistics," U.S. Department of Justice, December 31, 1996.

48) Spiros Zodhiates, Th.D., ed., *Hebrew-Greek Key Study Bible, King James Version* (World Bible Publishers, 1991), *Dictionary of the Greek Testament,* James Strong, S.T.D., L.L.D., No. 1074, p. 113.

49) *The World Almanac and Book of Facts 1998,* (K-III Reference Corporation, 1997), p. 176.

50) Ibid., pp. 174-175.

51) Ibid., p. 502.

> *...I will come again, and receive you to Myself; that where I am, there you may be also.*
>
> John 14:3

Chapter 4

The Rapture of the Church

Before the seven-year Tribulation begins, the Church, or the body of Christ, will be removed from the earth. By the "Church," we mean all who have sincerely invited Jesus into their hearts, those who truly have a relationship with Him. There are many professing Christians who never "bring forth fruit in keeping with repentance" (Matt. 3:8). They come to church on Sunday but do little, if anything, for the kingdom of God. They profess Christ with their mouths but not with their lives.

When someone has a true born-again experience, their life changes by the power of the Holy Spirit. There is no exception. No one comes to know the Lord, "or rather to be known by God" (Gal. 4:9), and remain in the condition they were before their profession of faith. That is not to say they will not sin or struggle with old sinful behavior, just as the apostle Paul did (Rom. 7:14-25), but there is a point at which all genuine believers can look back and identify when change began. Scripture is clear that "a man is justified by works, and not by faith alone" (James 2:24). Indeed, faith alone saves, but the faith that saves is not alone. Righteousness evidenced by good works *must* accompany faith if there be genuine salvation. "Was not Abraham our father justified by works, when he offered up Isaac his son on the altar? And in the same way, was not Rahab the harlot also justified by works, when she received the messengers and sent them out by another way?" (James 2:21, 25) When the Rapture happens, there will be many people still sitting in the pews, wondering why they were not taken. "Not everyone who says to Me, 'Lord, Lord,' will enter the kingdom of heaven; but he who does the will of My Father who is in heaven" (Matt. 7:21).

It is past the hour for us to stop playing church. If you have not already done so, now is the time to bend your knee before the Father and confess you are a sinner in need of a Savior, and ask Jesus to come into your heart and be the Lord and Master of your life. And if you ask Him with a sincere heart, you *will* begin to experience change, and you *will* bring forth fruit in keeping with repentance as a natural outpouring of your love and devotion to the Lord for what He has done for you. Do not be deceived into believing you are saved if you are not. Clearly, "faith without works is dead" (James 2:26).

When Jesus comes to receive the true Church unto Himself, the bodies of all believers who have died since the Day of Pentecost nearly 2,000 years ago will come forth from their graves and ascend to meet Jesus in the clouds where they will join with their spirits which come with Him from heaven. "For if we believe that Jesus died and rose again, even so God will bring with Him those who have fallen asleep in Jesus" (1 Thess. 4:14). The term "fallen asleep" means believers who have died.

The ascension of the Church to meet Jesus in the

clouds is called the Rapture, although nowhere in Scripture is it referred to by this title. When the Rapture occurs, Jesus will only come as far as the clouds, at which point, "The Lord Himself will descend from heaven with a shout, with the voice of the archangel, and with the trumpet of God; and the dead in Christ shall rise first. Then we who are alive and remain shall be caught up together with them in the clouds to meet the Lord in the air, and thus we shall always be with the Lord" (1 Thess. 4:16-17). In this passage, the Greek translation of the phrase "shall be caught up" is the word "harpazo," meaning "catch away." "Harpazo" is derived from the Greek word "haireomai," meaning "to take for oneself." In the fifth century, a Latin translation of the Greek phrase "caught up" was "rapere," and this translation formed the basis for our modern word "rapture." It involves *only* the Church-age saints, that is, all genuine believers who have placed their trust in the Lord Jesus from the Day of Pentecost forward to the Rapture.

In the parable of the rich man and Lazarus, Jesus revealed that when a believer dies, his spirit is carried away by angels to heaven (Luke 16:22). As well, Paul wrote, "to be absent from the body (is) to be at home with the Lord" (2 Cor. 5:8). Although at death our bodies are left to undergo decay, they will someday be resurrected to join with our spirits. For believers, there are different resurrection programs, which will be discussed in chronological order of Tribulation events. For the unbelieving dead, their spirits descend into Hades, or hell, where they will remain until their bodies are resurrected at the Great White Throne Judgment, which will occur at the conclusion of the Millennium.

Immediately after the dead in Christ rise to meet the Lord in the air, all believers who are *alive* at that time will instantly be transformed into a glorified state and also ascend to meet them in the clouds. "Behold, I tell you a mystery; we shall not all sleep, but we shall all be changed, in a moment, in the twinkling of an eye, at the last trumpet; for the trumpet will sound, and the dead will be raised imperishable, and we shall be changed" (1 Cor. 15:51-52). But believers who are living "shall not precede those who have fallen asleep" (1 Thess. 4:15).

After Christ's resurrection, He appeared to His disciples "over a period of forty days" (Acts 1:3). When He appeared to them, they could touch Him and feel His flesh, yet He could also walk through walls. Thomas, one of the disciples, was having difficulty believing Jesus was alive. He said to the other disciples, "Unless I shall see in His hands the imprint of the nails, and put my finger into the place of the nails, and put my hand into His side, I will not believe" (John 20:25). But eight days after making that statement, Scripture says, "Jesus came, the doors having been shut, and stood in their midst" (John 20:26). He turned to Thomas and said, "Reach here your finger, and see My hands; and reach here your hand, and put it into My side; and be not unbelieving, but believing" (John 20:27). Jesus was in a glorified state, the same condition into which believers will be changed "in the twinkling of an eye."

The Church is promised deliverance from the Tribulation. Throughout Scripture, God always removed the righteous before pouring out His wrath and judgment on the unrighteous. In the case of Noah, the "Lord saw that the wickedness of man was great on the earth, and that every intent of the thoughts of his heart was only evil continually. The Lord was sorry that He had made man on the earth, and He was grieved in His heart. But Noah found favor in the eyes of the

Lord" (see Gen. 6:5-6, 8). So God destroyed the earth and all its inhabitants with a flood, but removed Noah and his family from His wrath.

Again, in the case of righteous Lot, when two angels came to visit him in the city of Sodom, the men of the city came to his door and asked him to bring the angels out in order to have homosexual relations with them. Lot pleaded with the men to take his daughters instead, but they rushed him and were about to break in the door to get to them when the angels reached out and grabbed Lot, pulling him inside. The angels then told Lot to take his family and leave the city, that the Lord was going to destroy the cities of the valley "because their outcry has become so great before the Lord." But Lot hesitated, so the angels took him, his wife, and their two daughters and *physically* removed them from the city, and God "rained on Sodom and Gomorrah brimstone and fire" (see Gen. 19:1-29). Today, all that remains of the cities are high concentrations of salt where once they stood.

It is not God's plan to put his righteous children through the Tribulation. While some may argue against the righteousness of the Church, it is true the believer's "righteousness is as filthy rags" (Isa. 64:6), but when we receive Jesus into our hearts as Lord and Savior, we receive an imputed righteousness through Him so that when God looks at us, He does not see the person we are, but rather, the Person of Jesus Christ, whose shed blood covers our sins. As such, "having now been justified by His blood, we shall be saved from the wrath of God through Him" (Rom. 5:9).

In Revelation chapters 1 through 3, John is on earth viewing events around him from ground level. In chapter 4 he, as is the Church at the Rapture, is caught up to heaven where he is viewing earth's Tribulation from above. As such, his removal before events of the Tribulation are revealed to him, depicts the Church's removal before the Tribulation begins. Clearly, the purpose of the Tribulation is not to pour out wrath upon God's beloved children. Jesus has already taken God's wrath for us at the Cross. Jesus promised, "Because you have kept the word of My perseverance, I also will keep you from the hour of testing, that hour which is about to come upon the whole world, to test those who dwell upon the earth" (Rev. 3:10). Again, the apostle Paul urged us "to wait for...Jesus, who delivers us from the wrath to come," and that "God has not destined us for wrath, but for obtaining salvation through our Lord Jesus Christ" (1 Thess. 1:10; 5:9).

The Rapture is designed to remove the Church to heaven while God purges sin from the earth during the remaining seven years that follow. Jesus will then return to earth at the Second Advent, occurring at the conclusion of the seven-year Tribulation, to establish His righteous 1,000-year kingdom on earth. So sin must be reckoned with by the commencement of the Millennium. The Rapture and the Second Advent are two different events. This will become clearer as we progress.

There is no prophecy remaining to be fulfilled regarding the Rapture. It can happen at any moment, day or night. Paul encouraged the Church to keep "looking for the blessed hope and the appearing of the glory of our great God and Savior, Christ Jesus" (Titus 2:13).

What Happens to the Church After the Rapture?

Judgment Seat of Christ

Scripture says, "We must all appear before the judgment seat of Christ, that each one may be recompensed for his deeds in the body, according to what he has done, whether good or bad" (2 Cor. 5:10). At the Rapture, the Church is removed to heaven where we will stand before the Judgment Seat of Christ to receive our rewards for faithful service while on earth. This will occur for 3½ years and parallel the first half of the Tribulation occurring on earth.

Believers do not face judgment for sins committed during their lifetime. Our sins are completely forgiven at the very moment we receive Jesus as our Savior, including those we will commit after receiving Him. When He died on the cross, He paid the price for sin once and for all, and trusting in Him totally wipes our sin away, those committed in the past, the present, or those we will commit in the future. When we stand before Him at the Judgment Seat, it is solely to receive our rewards for service. "Therefore we have as our ambition...to be pleasing to Him" (2 Cor. 5:9).

Jesus laid the foundation for how we are to live, and after salvation, the believer becomes "God's fellow worker" in the kingdom (1 Cor. 3:9). As such, "each will receive his own reward according to his own labor" (1 Cor. 3:8). When we stand before the Judgment Seat, our works will be thrown into fire, "and the fire itself will test the quality of each man's work" (1 Cor. 3:13). If the work does not burn up, we will receive a reward. But "if any man's work is burned up, he shall suffer loss; but he himself shall be saved" (1 Cor. 3:15). How many of us will "suffer loss" before the Lord on that day?

> *I will give to each one of you according to your deeds.*
>
> Revelation 2:23

Marriage Supper of the Lamb

After receiving rewards for faithful servitude, the Church will then lay them at Jesus' feet and begin to celebrate the Marriage Supper of the Lamb in heaven for 3½ more years, which will parallel the Great Tribulation occurring on earth. The Church is depicted in Scripture as the Bride and Jesus, the Bridegroom. After the Judgment Seat, the Bridegroom will take His Bride unto Himself and consummate the relationship, that we may be united with Him eternally. When a man and woman are joined together in marriage, there is joy at the union of the two. Scripture says, "Husbands, love your wives, just as Christ also loved the church and gave Himself up for her; that He might sanctify her, having cleansed her by the washing of water with the word, that He might present to Himself the church in all her glory, having no spot or wrinkle or any such thing" (Eph. 5:25-27).

When Jesus unites with His beloved Bride in marriage, the two will experience pure, unspeakable joy, unlike any wedding night on this side of heaven and one which cannot be fully appreciated until that long-awaited day.

> *Blessed are those who are invited to the marriage supper of the Lamb.*
>
> Revelation 19:9

Chapter 5

The Players—Who's Who in the Tribulation

At the commencement of the Tribulation, the unveiling of prophecy will rapidly begin. There are a number of key figures and terms which must be identified before we can begin the chronology. Each of these persons or celestial beings will be characterized by who they are, what their role is, when they will appear, and for how long. It is important to keep in mind, while other events are taking place, these figures will fulfill their prophetical positions simultaneously.

The Holy Spirit

The Holy Spirit is God Himself living on the inside of us (John 14:16-17; 14:20; Rom. 8:11). For believers today, the work of the Spirit is to guide and lead us into the way of truth. He reproves and convicts of sin, and also helps us in our weaknesses, interceding on our behalf to the Father with groanings too deep for words (Rom. 8:26). He illuminates the Scriptures and calls to mind the things of Jesus (John 14:26). He is our Helper, our Teacher, our Comforter, our

Counselor, our Guide. But after the Rapture, His role will revert back to the days of the Old Testament.

As the third Person of the Holy Trinity, He is omniscient and omnipresent and will remain on the earth during the Tribulation. His position, however, will not be one of an indwelling ministry. To indwell believers would necessarily mean they are sealed, just as believers today are "sealed in Him with the Holy Spirit of promise" (Eph. 1:13) at the moment we receive Jesus as our Savior. But clearly, the 144,000 Jews who receive Jesus at the *beginning* of the Tribulation are sealed with the "seal of the living God" at the *midpoint*. These individuals are the only ones sealed during the Tribulation, though Scripture says, "A great multitude, which no one could count, from every nation and all tribes and peoples and tongues" (Rev. 7:9) will also receive salvation, for they are pictured standing "before the throne of God" (Rev. 7:15), wearing white robes that were washed in the blood of the Lamb. These martyred saints are not *sealed* by the Holy Spirit.

J. Dwight Pentecost put it this way: "Apart from the indwelling ministry, Old Testament saints were said to be saved by the Holy Spirit, even though He did not indwell that believer as a temple. So in the Tribulation, the Holy Spirit will do the work of regeneration as He did when God was previously dealing with Israel, but without an indwelling ministry. The present-day indwelling is related to empowerment, to union of believer with believer because of their relation to the Temple of God, but the indwelling is entirely distinct and separate from the work of the Spirit in regeneration."[1]

Therefore, the work of the Spirit during the Tribulation will solely be one of a regenerative nature. He will work to bring people to salvation, though not indwelling them. Just as salvation today is by faith, so will it be then, but prior to the Tribulation, believers have the indwelling Spirit "who is given as a pledge of our inheritance" (Eph. 1:14), thereafter guiding and enabling us to live victoriously over sin.

The Satanic Trinity

In the book of Revelation, we see the personages of the Satanic trinity. In chapter 12, Satan is depicted as the great red dragon and leader of the counterfeit trinity. In chapter 13, two beasts are depicted, one rising out of the sea; the other, a beast rising out of the earth. These beasts are the Antichrist and the False Prophet respectively.

In the counterfeit Satanic trinity, Satan will attempt to emulate God; the Antichrist will attempt to emulate Jesus by fulfilling a covenant, albeit a false one, regarding the peaceful occupation of Israel in their land; and the False Prophet will attempt to mirror the work of the Holy Spirit by pointing men to the Antichrist as God. Satan never creates; he only counterfeits and imitates.

Satan

There are many titles given to this wicked fallen angel. He is the chief adversary of God and man, and his only purpose is to thwart God's divine plan of grace through a facade of deception. He is a destroyer, a liar, referred to by Jesus as "the evil one" (Matt. 13:19, 38). The apostle Peter even warned believers to "be on the alert. Your adversary, the devil, prowls about like a roaring lion, seeking someone to devour" (1 Pet. 5:8).

Among Satan's many titles, the term "dragon" is most used in the book of Revelation in reference to him. "And the great dragon was thrown down, the serpent of old who is called the devil and Satan" (Rev. 12:9). The "dragon" terminology was used in the Old Testament to refer to those who persecuted the children of Israel. Pharaoh is referred to as "the great dragon." Scripture says, "...behold, I am against thee, Pharaoh king of Egypt, the great dragon that lieth in the midst of his rivers...." (Ezek. 29:3, KJV). As well, Nebuchadnezzar is likened to a "dragon" for his persecution of Israel. "Nebuchadnezzar the king of Babylon hath devoured me...he hath swallowed me up like a dragon" (Jer. 51:34, KJV). And so it is today. Persecution is a way of life for every child of God, and the more we try to live godly, the more persecution we face. The apostle Paul wrote, "Indeed, all who desire to live godly in Christ Jesus will be persecuted" (2 Tim. 3:12).

Satan is the ruler of this world. He is the cause of sin and rebellion. Jesus Himself referred to Satan three times as the "prince of the world," while Paul referred to him as the "god of this world." Satan will control the activity of the counterfeit trinity throughout the Tribulation, but he will physically indwell the body of the Antichrist at the midpoint.

The Antichrist

In the Scriptures, there are approximately thirty titles given to the Antichrist. The name Antichrist is derived from the word "anti," meaning "against," coupled with his activity in the Satanic trinity paralleling that of Christ's in the

Godhead. During the Tribulation, he will be "anti-Christ," emulating a Christlike persona of peace, yet completely against God and His Son.

Among his many titles, he is referred to as the beast, the wicked one, the violent man, the Assyrian, the spoiler, the little horn, the wilful king, the man of sin, the son of perdition, the lawless one, the desolator, and the head of many countries, to name a few.

The prophet Daniel recorded in detail events surrounding the "time of the end" when the Antichrist would emerge. These will be revealed as we progress chronologically. He also recorded specific information regarding the Antichrist himself. Daniel described him as large in appearance, having a fierce countenance (Dan. 7:20; 8:23, KJV). He will be skilled in speech and powerful, though not by his own power (Dan. 8:23-24). He will speak blasphemous words against Almighty God, having no regard for Him or the desire of women (Rev. 13:5; Dan. 11:36-37, KJV). He will also perform signs and false wonders (2 Thess. 2:9).

The Antichrist will not appear until the Church is Raptured. At the beginning of the Tribulation, he will emerge out of a ten-nation European alliance and bring peace to Israel. He will be extremely well-liked by all the nations and ultimately elevated to world ruler by the midpoint of the Tribulation, possessing "authority over every tribe and people and tongue and nation" (Rev. 13:7). Scripture says, "All who dwell on the earth will worship him, everyone whose name has not been written from the foundation of the world in the book of life of the Lamb who has been slain" (Rev. 13:8). He will rule the world for 3½ years, from the second half of the Tribulation onward. "Authority to act for forty-two months was given to him" (Rev. 13:5; 12:14; Dan. 7:25).

Though the Antichrist emerges at the beginning of the Tribulation, his true evil persona will not be manifested until Satan physically indwells his body at the midpoint and onward to its end. Throughout the Tribulation, however, the Antichrist will be the key figure in the Satanic trinity. He will be guided by Satan during the first half and possessed by him in the second. When the devil indwells the Antichrist, the Great Tribulation will begin; the "time of Jacob's trouble." It will be a time of distress "such as never occurred since there was a nation until that time" (Dan. 12:2). Scripture warns, "Woe to the earth and the sea, because the devil has come down to you, having great wrath, knowing that he has only a short time" (Rev. 12:12). At that point, the Antichrist will begin his slaughter of the Jews and of those who accept Jesus as Lord after the Rapture.

Contrary to popular belief, the Antichrist will be a nonobservant Jew. In Revelation 7, a divine seal is placed on the foreheads of 144,000 Jews, 12,000 from each of the twelve tribes of Israel. This takes place at the midpoint of the Tribulation to protect them from the Antichrist's persecution during the latter half. However, the tribe of Dan is omitted. They are not sealed and will not be protected by God. While no one knows for sure why this is so, a popular belief is because of their many idolatrous acts throughout Jewish history. But a better explanation may be found in the Antichrist being a descendant from this tribe. God will not protect the tribe of Dan because one of their members will be possessed by Satan, who will slaughter millions of Jews.

Scripture says, "Dan shall be a serpent in the way, a horned snake in the path" (Gen. 49:17). Since the Antichrist will likely come from the tribe of Dan, the characterization of Dan as a "serpent" may be seen in the Antichrist's federation with Satan, who is referred to as the serpent. In this same passage, the King James refers to the "horned snake" as an adder. This serpent is a venomous viper found in the region of the Near East, or Europe, where the Antichrist will emerge. And Daniel used a like description in referring to the Antichrist as "the little horn."

Another reason why we believe him to be a Jew is because Daniel recorded, "Neither shall he regard the God of his fathers" (Dan. 11:37, KJV). The phrase "God of his fathers" is a common phrase used no less than 48 times in the Scriptures by the Jews when referring to God. In other words, the Jewish Antichrist will have no regard for his God.

Finally, while most of the Jews still await their Messiah, when a man emerges with miraculous powers, bringing peace to Israel, and a religious figure who also performs many miracles proclaims the man of peace to actually be God, the Jews will be convinced he is their long-awaited Messiah. They would not accept him as such if he were not a Jew. Jesus said, "I have come in My Father's name, and you do not receive Me; if another shall come in his own name, you will receive him" (John 5:43).

Parenthetically, when the Jews were dispersed in the Diaspora, the descendants of the tribe of Dan migrated in a northwesterly direction, mainly into the Balkan area. As they settled, to remain true to their heritage, they named many locations after their ancestral father, Dan, oftentimes using his name as a root form. For example, there is the Danube River which runs through the Balkan States. They also retained the name throughout their ancestry, much as we do today in naming our children after a parent or grandparent. It is interesting to note the key writer on the Antichrist is Daniel, whose ancestry is unidentified. This in no way implies Daniel was evil; in fact, we know that he was exceedingly godly. But by Daniel writing about the Antichrist, who will come from the tribe of Dan, we see the mystery and magnificence of God, who reveals truth to the honest seeker, and we know there are no coincidences with Him.

The Antichrist will emerge at the onset of the Tribulation and remain until Jesus returns to earth at the end of the Tribulation. Though Scripture says the beast will suffer a fatal head wound and his head is then healed (Rev. 13:3, 12, 14), this is symbolic of the revived Roman Empire and should not be misinterpreted as a resurrection of the Antichrist. The beast is seen coming out of the sea, having seven heads and ten horns (Rev. 13:1). One of the seven heads suffers a fatal wound, but later we see that the seven heads are seven kings (Rev. 17:10). Therefore, a more likely explanation is that the seven heads depict the seven world empires in the Bible, to include Egypt, Assyria, Babylon, Medo-Persia, Greece, and Rome. The head which suffers a mortal wound and then comes to life depicts Rome and, thereafter, the revived Roman Empire. Finally, Satan has no power to give life, and try as he might, he cannot resurrect anyone. So if the Antichrist died, he would stay dead.

The False Prophet

Jesus said, "If anyone says to you, 'Behold, here is the Christ,' or 'There He is,' do not believe him" (Matt. 24:23). Shortly before the midpoint of the Tribulation while the Antichrist is rising in power, the False Prophet will emerge. As the third component of the Satanic trinity, he will attempt to emulate the ministry of the Holy Spirit in the Godhead. Just as the Holy Spirit directs believers in the worship of Jesus

Christ, the False Prophet will direct the world into the worship of the Antichrist. "He makes the earth and those who dwell in it to worship the first beast" (Rev. 13:12). Because he is depicted as a lamb, he will likely be or have been a religious figure (Rev. 13:11).

Over 1600 years ago, the prophet Malachi told of the appearance of Elijah before the coming day of the Lord. Because most Jews do not believe their Messiah has come, they continue to await the arrival of Elijah to herald the approach of their Messiah. Indeed, Elijah *will* appear at the beginning of the Tribulation, but as one of the Two Witnesses of God. He will not be recognized by the Jews, for he will be a prophet of judgment, exacting punishment for 3½ years during the first half of the Tribulation in an effort to turn men's hearts to repentance.

Knowing the Jews await the appearance of Elijah to precede Christ, the False Prophet will seize the opportunity for deception, sporting a profile of Elijah the Jews will accept. 2 Kings 1:1-16 reveals the account of Elijah causing fire to rain down from heaven, consuming King Ahaziah's messengers. The king fell through lattice in his upper chamber, and as a result of his injuries, became seriously ill. As such, he sent messengers to Elijah to determine whether he would recover. But because he initially sought the advice of a foreign god, Elijah was granted authority to destroy the messengers by raining fire down from heaven and consuming them. The False Prophet will have the same power. "He performs great signs, so that he even makes fire come down out of heaven to the earth in the presence of men" (Rev. 13:13). The Jews are intimately familiar with Elijah's record of miracles, and as such, they will believe the False Prophet is Elijah. Because Malachi warned Elijah would precede the

Lord, when the False Prophet claims the man who secured Israel's peace in his initial rise to world power is indeed their long-awaited Messiah, the Jews will believe it.

The two will exhibit miraculous power. Jesus warned of this. "False Christs and false prophets will arise and will show great signs and wonders, so as to mislead, if possible, even the elect" (Matt. 24:24). The False Prophet will be limited in his ability to perform miracles. His power will only operate in the presence of the Antichrist. "He deceives those who dwell on the earth because of the signs which it was given him to perform in the presence of the beast" (Rev. 13:14).

The False Prophet will administer the worldwide Mark of the Beast system beginning at the midpoint of the Tribulation. "He causes all, the small and the great, and the rich and the poor, and the free men and the slaves, to be given a mark on their right hand, or on their forehead, and he provides that no one should be able to buy or to sell, except the one who has the mark, either the name of the beast or the number of his name" (Rev. 13:16-17).

Once the False Prophet emerges, sometime within the first half of the Tribulation, he will remain until Jesus returns to earth at the end of the Tribulation.

The 144,000 Jewish Witnesses

After the Church is removed at the Rapture, God will turn His attention to the nation of Israel. By a supernatural occurrence, 144,000 Jews scattered throughout the world will receive salvation, 12,000 from each of the twelve tribes of Israel, except Dan (Rev. 7:1-8). In Dan's place is the tribe of Levi, who are not usually included when reference is made to the twelve tribes of Israel. They were set apart by God for priestly service, and therefore He was their inheritance (Deut. 10:9). Though the tribe of Dan will not be divinely sealed during the Tribulation, they will be restored to inhabit the northernmost region of Israel during Christ's millennial reign on earth (Ezek. 48:1).

The origin of the twelve tribes of Israel is recorded in the book of Genesis, beginning with the life of Jacob. Chapter 30 reveals the twelve sons who were born to him. Then in chapter 35, God changed Jacob's name to Israel. Each of Israel's (Jacob) twelve sons became fathers, and their descendants became what is known as the twelve "tribes" of Israel, the Israelites. Each descending tribe was named after their ancestral father, one of Israel's sons.

No one knows what supernatural event will cause the 144,000 Jews to accept Jesus as their Savior, but throughout the Tribulation, they will preach to the world of the coming Messiah. It appears the Spirit of God moves sovereignly to bring about their conversion. Just as the apostle Paul "saw the light" when he encountered the Lord on the road to Damascus (Acts 26), something miraculous will occur in the lives of these 144,000 Jews. Paul's conversion to Christ represents a prototype of what the 144,000 Jews will experience. Their ministry will be worldwide, and the effect of their message will result in "a great multitude, which no one could count" (Rev. 7:9), repenting and accepting Jesus as their Savior.

The Two Witnesses of God

At the beginning of the Tribulation, two men dressed in sackcloth will appear in Israel, preaching judgment and repentance, for the coming of the Lord is at hand. Sackcloth is a black garment made of angora goat hair, usually worn over another garment as a symbol of judgment. It was worn during Old Testament days by mourners and prophets.

Speculation abounds as to the identity of these two men. Some believe them to be Elijah and Moses; others believe them to be Elijah and Enoch; while still others believe them to be only spiritual representations of the Old Testament prophets.

However, regarding the identity of the first witness, Jesus said, "Elijah is coming and will restore all things" (Matt. 17:11). As well, the prophet Malachi foretold the appearance of Elijah before the Lord returns. "Behold, I am going to send My messenger, and he will clear the way before Me" (Mal. 3:1). This is not to be confused with John the Baptist, because the following verse says, "But who can endure the day of His coming? And who can stand when He appears?" (Mal. 3:2) This is an obvious reference to the time preceding Christ's second coming to earth. Malachi then clears up any confusion as to the timing of Elijah's appearance. "Behold, I am going to send you Elijah the prophet before the coming of the great and terrible day of the Lord" (Mal. 4:5). And Jesus Himself confirmed, "Elijah is coming...." (Matt. 17:11).

Elijah was the preeminent prophet of judgment. Just as Elijah prayed and stopped the rain for 3½ years (1 Kin. 17:1), the Two Witnesses will possess the same power, also stopping the rain for 3½ years. "I will grant authority to My two witnesses, and they will prophecy twelve hundred and sixty days, clothed in sackcloth. These have the power to shut up the sky, in order that rain may not fall during the days of their prophesying" (Rev. 11:3, 6).

A strong argument may also be made for Elijah's identity as one of the Two Witnesses because he did not experience physical death. He was transported into heaven in his physical body. "Then it came about as they were going along and talking, that behold, there appeared a chariot of fire and horses of fire which separated the two of them. And Elijah went up by a whirlwind to heaven" (2 Kin. 2:11). Because the prophet did not die, this possibly suggests God carried him to heaven to someday place him back on the earth as one of the two prophets of judgment, who will then experience death.

But most of the speculation surrounding the Two Witnesses lies in the identity of the second witness. Clearly, Elijah is the first. However, strong argument is made for both Enoch or Moses as the second witness.

Enoch, like Elijah, was a prophet of judgment. Jude referenced Enoch's prophecy regarding the return of Christ. He wrote, "Behold, the Lord came with many thousands of His holy ones, to execute judgment upon all, and to convict all the ungodly of all their ungodly deeds which they have done in an ungodly way, and of all the harsh things which ungodly sinners have spoken against Him" (Jude 14-15). Enoch also did not experience physical death. "And Enoch walked with God; and he was not, for God took him" (Gen. 5:24). This possibly suggests he will be the second prophet of judgment.

However, Moses was the man used by God to establish the Law for Israel. Jesus said, "Do not think that I came to abolish the Law or the Prophets; I did not come to abolish, but to fulfill" (Matt. 5:17). Therefore, because the Law came through Moses, he also is a likely candidate for the second witness. As well, Moses turned water into blood and smote the land of Egypt with plagues (Ex. 7:14-21). The Two Witnesses will do the same. "They have the power over the waters to turn them into blood, and to smite the earth with every plague, as often as they desire" (Rev. 11:6).

Finally, and perhaps the most popular reason the second witness is believed to be Moses, is he stood with Elijah and Jesus on the Mount of Transfiguration, discussing Christ's imminent death. Because of this, it is therefore held he will appear with Elijah to announce Christ's imminent return.

Whoever the Two Witnesses are, their ministry will be confined to the nation of Israel. They will appear immediatly after the Rapture and remain throughout the first half of the Tribulation, preaching a message of judgment and repentance. Anyone who attempts to harm them will be killed instantly by fire, which will proceed out of their mouths. "And if anyone desires to harm them, fire proceeds out of their mouth and devours their enemies" (Rev. 11:5). Their ministry will last exactly 1,260 days (Rev. 11:3), not one day more or less. When their time is complete, God will allow their deaths.

The Three Angels

During His Olivet Discourse, Jesus said, "This gospel of the kingdom shall be preached in the whole world for a witness to all the nations, and then the end shall come" (Matt. 24:14). This verse has been the catalyst for today's worldwide evangelistic revival in hopes of delaying no longer the return of Christ. While evangelizing is certainly commanded in the Great Commission (Matt. 28:19-20; Mark 16:15), the days have been allotted until the time of the end, and they will not be expedited by man's evangelizing efforts.

In fact, the final spreading of the gospel to the whole world will not be by human agency, but rather, the work of the first of three angels flying in midheaven, who will appear at the midpoint and into the second half of the Tribulation preceding Christ's return to earth. "I saw another angel flying in midheaven, having an eternal gospel to preach to those who live on the earth, and to every nation and tribe and tongue and people; and he said with a loud voice, 'Fear God, and give Him glory, because the hour of His judgment has come; and worship Him who made the heaven and the earth and sea and springs of waters'" (Rev. 14:6-7).

The second angel follows behind the first, saying, "Fallen, fallen is Babylon the great, she who has made all the nations drink of the wine of the passion of her immorality" (Rev. 14:8). This refers to the nations of the world being deceived by the false religious system, accepting the testimony of the False Prophet in worshiping the Antichrist as God.

The third angel follows behind the first two angels "saying with a loud voice, 'If anyone worships the beast and his image, and receives a mark on his forehead or upon his hand, he also will drink of the wine of the wrath of God, which is mixed in full strength in the cup of His anger; and he will be tormented with fire and brimstone in the presence of the holy angels and in the presence of the Lamb. And the smoke of their torment goes up forever and ever; and they have no rest day and night, those who worship the beast and his image, and whoever receives the mark of his name'" (Rev. 14:9-11).

Endnotes

1) J. Dwight Pentecost, *Things to Come,* (Zondervan Publishing House, Grand Rapids, Michigan, 1958) p. 271.

Chapter 6

The Seals, Trumpets, and Bowls of Wrath

Before we can fully understand the seals, trumpets, and bowls of wrath, we must look at the scroll which the seven seals surround. It is not a coincidence that a similar scroll appears several times in the Scriptures and then appears a final time in Revelation 5 as the scroll Jesus opens to begin judgment during the Tribulation.

As we proceed with the seals, trumpets, and bowls of wrath, this chapter may seem somewhat complicated. It would be very helpful to the reader to actually refer to the Bible passages stated herein. In so doing, you will better grasp the correlations given.

The Scroll

We begin with the prophet Jeremiah. Before Jeremiah wrote his scroll, God told him, "'Stand in the court of the Lord's house, and speak to all the cities of Judah, who have come to worship in the Lord's house, all the words that I have commanded you to speak to them. Do not omit a word! Perhaps they will listen and everyone will turn from his evil way, that I may repent of the calamity which I am planning to do to them because of the evil of their deeds. And you will say to them, 'Thus says the Lord, 'If you will not listen to Me, to walk in My law, which I have set before you, to listen to the words of My servants the prophets, whom I have been sending to you again and again, but you have not listened; then I will make this house like Shiloh, and this city I will make a curse to all the nations of the earth''' (Jer. 26:3-6).

Jeremiah did as he was told, and afterward, the Lord instructed him again, saying, "Take a scroll and write on it all the words which I have spoken to you concerning Israel, and concerning Judah, and concerning all the nations, from the day I first spoke to you, from the days of Josiah, even to this day. Perhaps the house of Judah will hear all the calamity which I plan to bring on them, in order that every man will turn from his evil way; then I will forgive their iniquity and their sin" (Jer. 36:2-3).

Likewise, he did as the Lord instructed, and when it was all said and done, the scroll contained 23 years of Jeremiah's exhortation of Israel to repent or suffer complete destruction (Jer. 25). It was read aloud twice to the Jews, once in the Temple court and once before the Jewish princes. We do not know what was written on the scroll, but whatever it contained, Scripture says, "When they had heard all the words, they turned in fear one to another" (Jer. 36:16). It was then partially read to Judah's King Jehoiakim, who cut it up and burned it. Thereafter, the Lord instructed Jeremiah to rewrite the scroll verbatim (Jer. 36:28), which he did, "and many similar words were added" (Jer. 36:32). Jeremiah wept and lamented for his people, but they continued in their rebellion toward God.

The Lord then called the prophet Ezekiel to exhort the

Jews to repentance, and a scroll was handed to him, which appears to be the same scroll Jeremiah rewrote after King Jehoiakim burned it, possibly including the book of Lamentations as the "many similar words" he added to the scroll. The book of Lamentations was written by Jeremiah, which contains five poems of mourning for the destruction of Jerusalem. Scripture indicates the scroll handed to Ezekiel "was written on the front and back; and written on it were lamentations, mourning and woe" (Ezek. 2:10). Indeed, their failure to heed the warnings resulted in the destruction of Jerusalem at the hands of the Babylonians in 586 B.C., then again in 70 A.D. at the hands of the Romans, and it will occur a final time during the second half of the Tribulation surrounding the "woe" trumpet judgments and bowls of wrath.

It appears this same scroll "concerning Israel, and concerning Judah, and concerning all the nations" (Jer. 36:2) is recorded yet again in the Scriptures by the prophet Zechariah, who sees the scroll in a vision. This time it is flying unrolled in midair, measuring 30 feet long and 15 feet wide. Zechariah is told the scroll is "the curse that goeth forth over the face of the whole earth" (Zech. 5:1-3, KJV), which coincides with Jeremiah's words in which Israel will be a "curse to all the nations of the earth" (Jer. 26:6). The prophet Isaiah also wrote, "A curse devours the earth, and those who live in it are held guilty. Therefore, the inhabitants of the earth are burned, and few men are left" (Isa. 24:6).

Finally, in Revelation 5, we see what again appears to be the same scroll. While in exile on the tiny island of Patmos, John the apostle was given the vision of end-time events as revealed in the book of Revelation. In ancient days, scrolls were customarily written on one side only, yet the scroll handed to Ezekiel, the flying scroll Zechariah saw, and the scroll in

Revelation 5 were all written on the front and back, except the scroll in Revelation 5 now has seven seals around it.

Archaeologists have discovered thousands of seals dating back 4,000 years before Christ. A seal was a specially crafted device characterized by an insignia, usually made of metal or precious stones and shaped into finger rings. When an item was to be sealed, soft clay or melted wax would be placed on the item. The seal was then pressed into the clay or wax, bearing its insignia. Among their several uses, seals were placed over important books and documents which were to remain closed.

The Lord knew Israel would not repent at the exhortations of Jeremiah and Ezekiel, so following their respective ministries, he used another man to reveal Israel's ultimate fate. While in Babylonian captivity, a panoramic future of the Jewish nation was revealed to Daniel by the angel Gabriel (Dan. 9:24-26). Later, Daniel saw a terrifying vision of "great conflict" and was told the vision pertains to the Jews in the latter days (Dan. 10:1, 10:14). A lengthy explanation was given to Daniel concerning Israel's "great conflict," and afterwards, he was instructed to "seal up the book until the end of time" (Dan. 12:4). However, it was not the words in the book of Daniel that were to be sealed, but rather, the *vision* Daniel saw regarding Israel in the latter days. Isaiah had a similar experience with his prophetical end-time visions. Scripture says, "The entire vision shall be to you like the words of a sealed book" (Isa. 29:11), or "ciphrah" in the Hebrew, meaning scroll. When Daniel asked, "What will be the outcome of these events?" the angel responded, "Go your way, Daniel, for these words are concealed and sealed up until the end time" (Dan. 12:8-9).

Therefore, with the original scroll written by Jeremiah

regarding the fate of Israel and the world for failing to repent, which was then handed to Ezekiel to proclaim the same message, along with Zechariah's vision of the scroll being a curse going forth over the whole earth, all these descriptions of the scroll combined with Daniel's vision of Israel's future instructed to be sealed up until the end of time, it appears events in his panoramic vision of Israel *are* the seven seals around the scroll depicting the events of the Tribulation regarding Israel's "great conflict," which will also involve all the nations of the world. It is important to remember that with the removal of the Church at the Rapture, God will redirect His attention to Israel for the remaining seven years, and *they* are the focus of the Tribulation.

In Revelation 5, God is sitting on His throne holding the scroll in His right hand. The Lord Jesus then comes forth to take the scroll from God, and He begins to break it open, one seal at a time.

The Seals: Four Horsemen of the Apocalypse

Perhaps one of the most common misunderstandings of the seven-year Tribulation is that of the seal, trumpet, and bowl judgments. There are seven components to each judgment, that is, seven seals, seven trumpets, and seven bowls of wrath. However, contrary to popular belief, they do not happen in succession, but rather, they overlap and coincide throughout the Tribulation. For example, the seal judgments provide an *overview* of the *entire* Tribulation period, with the trumpet and bowl judgments depicted within the seals. As well, the last three trumpets coincide with the bowls of wrath during the Great Tribulation, or the second 3½ years. As I explain the seals, trumpets, and bowls, I will establish their point of origin in the Tribulation.

Six of the seven seal judgments are recorded in Revelation 6. As stated, the seals are an overview of the entire Tribulation. The first four seals reveal the Four Horsemen of the Apocalypse. As riders, they are symbolic of what is to transpire on the earth, again bearing in mind that Israel is the focus of the Tribulation.

John writes of the first horseman, "And I looked, and behold, a white horse, and he who sat on it had a bow; and a crown was given to him; and he went out conquering, and to conquer" (Rev. 6:2). It has long been held the first horseman depicts the Antichrist because he is seen riding a white horse, which symbolizes peace, while wearing a crown and carrying a bow with no arrows, indicating his false agenda. He is also seen going forth to conquer. There are others who believe the first horseman depicts Jesus Himself *because* of the white horse and crown the rider is given. However, the First Horseman of the Apocalypse may well represent, instead, the 144,000 Jews who evangelize throughout the Tribulation period.

When we take a closer look at this passage, we see a parallel to the white horse found in Revelation 19. In this passage, the riders on white horses are the Lord Jesus and the Raptured saints returning to the battle of Armageddon (Rev. 19:11, 14). Though they return to battle, none of the saints possess any weapons of warfare, indicating the victory has already been won at the Cross. When the 144,000 Jews begin evangelizing at the beginning of the Tribulation, they are seen carrying a bow with no arrows because they are going forth with the Word of God, which *is* their weapon of warfare. The Psalmist wrote, "If a man does not repent, He will sharpen His sword; He has bent His bow and made it ready" (Ps. 7:12).

And the apostle Paul tells us, "The sword of the Spirit...is the Word of God" (Eph. 6:17).

The fact that the first horseman has a bow with no arrows cannot in and of itself link this rider to the Antichrist because there are 37 other references in Scripture to bows with no arrows, and in five passages, God Himself provides an arrow. "For I will bend Judah as My bow...then the Lord will appear over them, and His arrow will go forth like lightning" (Zech. 9:13, 14). And "God will shoot at them with an arrow" (Ps. 64:7). Therefore, a more likely explanation for the bow with no arrows may be the Word of God and the message of salvation going forth from the 144,000 Jews.

Also, the first horseman is seen wearing a crown. Upon salvation, believers are given a crown. Once the 144,000 Jews are converted, they too will receive a crown. Jesus said, "I am coming quickly; hold fast what you have, in order that no one take your crown" (Rev. 3:11).

Finally, we see the first horseman going forth "conquering, and to conquer." The definition for "conquer" means "to overcome." At the beginning of the Tribulation, the 144,000 Jewish witnesses will preach to the world of its need for salvation and the coming of Christ. *They* are the ones who will go forth "conquering, and to conquer," and those who receive salvation are the ones who overcome the perils of the Tribulation by holding on to their faith. Scripture says, "Whatever is born of God overcomes the world; and this is the victory that has overcome the world—our faith" (1 John 5:4). The only other reference, or any derivation thereof, to the word "conquer" in the King James Version of the Bible is found in Romans 8:37 where it says believers "overwhelmingly conquer through Him who loved us."

Therefore, the first seal, being the First Horsman of

the Apocalypse, likely depicts the 144,000 Jewish evangelists. This seal, and the message of the gospel, will span the entirety of the Tribulation. Ultimately these Jews will enter into the Millennium in their physical bodies, having been instrumental in bringing "a great multitude, which no one could count, from every nation and all tribes and peoples and tongues" (Rev. 7:9) to salvation.

The Second Horseman of the Apocalypse is "granted to take peace from the earth, and that men should slay one another; and a great sword was given to him" (Rev. 6:3-4). The red color of this horse depicts bloodshed. While some believe this seal represents war, it more likely refers to the Antichrist's worldwide persecution of the Jews and believers throughout the second half of the Tribulation. During the first half, there will be a false peace on earth, but with the second horseman, peace will be removed at the midpoint when the Antichrist betrays Israel. At that point, men will indeed slay one another, just as the second seal depicts. Jesus warned, "An hour is coming for everyone who kills you to think that he is offering service to God" (John 16:2). He said, "Brother will deliver up brother to death, and a father his child; and children will rise up against parents, and cause them to be put to death." He added, "Do not think that I came to bring peace on the earth; I did not come to bring peace, but a sword" (Matt. 10:21, 10:34), in fact, a "great sword," as is given the second horseman. This second seal is placed in time beginning at the midpoint of the Tribulation and continuing throughout the second half, overlapping the "woe" trumpet judgments and the bowls of wrath.

The Third Horseman of the Apocalypse produces famine (Rev. 6:5-6). The black color of this horse depicts disease and resultant death. This seal obviously coincides with the ministry of the Two Witnesses of God in Israel during the first half of the Tribulation. They are given the power "to shut up the sky, in order that rain may not fall during the days of their prophesying...and to smite the earth with every plague, as often as they desire" (Rev. 11:6). Ezekiel recorded a third of Israel will die by plague or be consumed by famine (Ezek. 5:12). The ministry of the Two Witnesses will last exactly 1,260 days, until the midpoint of the Tribulation.

The Fourth Horseman of the Apocalypse brings forth death (Rev. 6:7-8). His horse is pale in color. The Greek word for "pale" is "chloros," meaning a sickly yellowish-green color. From "chloros," the English word "chlorine" is derived. In fact, chlorine is a heavy yellow-green gas. This seal likely depicts the War of Gog and Magog, which will occur shortly before the midpoint of the Tribulation. The prophet Ezekiel warned of this war nearly 2600 years ago (Ezek. 38-39). As the seals provide an overview of the entire Tribulation, the destruction of a third of the earth as revealed in the first four trumpets (Rev. 8:6-12) coincide with the devastation of the fourth seal. Chemical warfare will be a likely component of this war, which may explain the pale-colored horse.

In this fourth seal judgment, this rider is called Death; and Hades follows him. "Authority was given to them over a fourth of the earth, to kill with sword, and with famine, and with pestilence, and by the wild beasts of the earth" (Rev. 6:8). When we look at the War of Gog and Magog in Ezekiel, we see the same perilous conditions. God said, "Every man's sword will be against his brother. And with pestilence and with blood I shall enter into judgment with him. I shall give you as food to every kind of predatory bird and beast of the field" (Ezek. 38:21-22; 39:4). Again, this seal coincides with the first four trumpet judgments of Revelation 8, beginning shortly before the midpoint of the Tribulation.

The fifth seal depicts the Tribulation martyrs (Rev. 6:9-11). They are dressed in white robes (vs. 11) and pictured underneath the altar in heaven, having "been slain because of the word of God, and because of the testimony which they had maintained" (Rev. 6:9). The persecution of believers does not take place until the second half of the Tribulation. "These who are clothed in white robes...are the ones who come out of the great tribulation" (Rev. 7:13-14). Therefore, this seal overlaps in time with the conditions surrounding the "woe" trumpet judgments and the bowls of wrath.

The sixth seal depicts the campaign of Armageddon (Rev. 6:12-17), and coincides with the last three trumpets and the seven bowls of wrath, which all relate to Armageddon (Rev. 9, 16.) This seal warns of a "great earthquake" in which "every mountain and island were moved out of their places" (Rev. 6:14). Likewise, the seventh bowl of wrath warns of a "great earthquake" where "every island fled away, and the mountains were not found" (Rev. 16:20).

In the sixth seal, "the sky was split apart like a scroll when it is rolled up" (Rev. 6:14). Isaiah used the same description in reference to Armageddon when all the armies of the world converge on Israel. He writes, "For the Lord's indignation is against all the nations, and His wrath against all their armies. He has utterly destroyed them...the mountains will be drenched with their blood. All the host of heaven will wear away, and the sky will be rolled up like a scroll" (Isa. 34:2-4).

John says in the sixth seal, "The sun became black as sackcloth made of hair, and the whole moon became like blood" (Rev. 6:12). The prophet Joel recorded the same scene before Jesus returns to earth at the battle of Armageddon. He wrote, "I will display wonders in the sky and on the earth, blood, fire, and columns of smoke. The sun will be turned into darkness, and the moon into blood, before the great and awesome day of the Lord comes" (Joel 2:30-31).

Finally, the sixth seal describes the kings of the earth hiding themselves in caves, crying out to the mountains to fall on them and to hide them "from the presence of Him who sits on the throne, and from the wrath of the Lamb; for the great day of their wrath has come; and who is able to stand?" (Rev. 6:16-17) This coincides with the seventh trumpet, where the temple of God in heaven is opened up. These men actually see God in the sky seated on His throne (Rev. 11:19), which is why they are seen running and hiding. At that point, Jesus returns in wrath to slay them (Rev. 11:18; 19:21). I believe the sky opening up to reveal God in His temple is the sign Jesus spoke of that would appear in the sky before He returned to earth (Matt. 24:30).

Therefore, this sixth seal is placed in time at the conclusion of the Tribulation and coincides with the campaign of Armageddon as revealed in the last three trumpets and all seven bowls of wrath.

The seventh and final seal produces the seven trumpet judgments (Rev. 8).

The Trumpets

The trumpet judgments are recorded in Revelation 8, 9, and 11:15-19. As mentioned, they are incorporated within the seal judgments, but they provide more insight into the devastating conditions on earth during the Tribulation. The first four begin just prior to the midpoint, while the last three span the second half and are commonly referred to as the "woe" judgments. The trumpets are highly symbolic and characterize the ravages of warfare. We must bear in mind the prophetical writers could only describe what they saw to the best of their ability, while we have the benefit of understanding their visions based on the development of weapons which match their description.

At the sounding of the first trumpet, a third of the earth, a third of the trees, and all the green grass is burned up. At the second trumpet, a "great mountain burning with fire (is) thrown into the sea" (Rev. 8:8), and a third of the sea turns to blood, killing a third of the creatures in the sea and also destroying a third of the ships. Notice the reference to "sea" and not "seas," plural. This likely represents the Mediterranean Sea, the sea of the Bible. At the third trumpet, a great star called "Wormwood" is seen falling from heaven, burning "like a torch." It falls on the rivers and springs of waters, making them bitter. At the fourth trumpet, a third of the sun, moon, and stars are darkened.

These first four trumpets are placed in time just shortly before the midpoint of the Tribulation and befit the carnage described in Ezekiel 38 and 39 surrounding the War of Gog and Magog. The fourth seal judgment and the first four trumpets coincide with each other.

Recalling the fourth seal, authority is given to kill over a fourth of the earth's population, yet with the first four trumpets, a third of the earth is destroyed. The War of Gog and Magog will involve a number of Middle Eastern Arab nations, Israel, Russia, Eastern Europe, and several countries in Northern Africa. When we look at a world map, this region clearly comprises a third of the earth. Likewise, this densely populated region could account for a quarter of the world's population, or 1.5 billion people.

The remaining three trumpets are referred to as the

"woe" judgments because of the eagle which flies in midheaven, saying, "Woe, woe, woe to those who dwell on the earth, because of the remaining blasts of the trumpet of the three angels who are about to sound!" (Rev. 8:13) They begin at the midpoint, commencing the Great Tribulation. Jesus warned, "There will be a great tribulation, such as has not occurred since the beginning of the world until now, nor ever shall. And unless those days had been cut short, no life would have been saved" (Matt. 24:21-22).

The fifth and sixth trumpets are incorporated within the sixth seal and also parallel the seven bowls of wrath. They depict the horrors beginning at the midpoint and into the second half of the Tribulation, the Great Tribulation. When Satan indwells the body of the Antichrist at the midpoint of the Tribulation, he begins his worldwide slaughter. Scripture says, "Woe to the earth and the sea, because the devil has come down to you, having great wrath, knowing that he has only a short time" (Rev. 12:12). At that point, only 1,260 days remain in the Tribulation. Satan hates God and all who belong to Him, and for the remaining 3½ years, he unleashes his fury on God's beloved children. "And when the dragon (Satan) saw that he was thrown down to the earth, he persecuted the woman (Israel) who gave birth to the male child. And the dragon was enraged with the woman, and went off to make war with the rest of her offspring, who keep the commandments of God and hold to the testimony of Jesus" (Rev. 12:13, 12:17, parentheses mine).

With the sounding of the fifth trumpet, the first of three "woe" judgments, Satan will physically possess the body of the Antichrist for the remainder of the Tribulation. As such, he is the preeminent force in bringing complete and total world chaos. He immediately opens the pit of hell and locusts are unleashed on the earth. They are "not permitted to kill anyone, but to torment for five months; and their torment was like the torment of a scorpion when it stings a man" (Rev. 9:5). The pain and anguish inflicted by this judgment will cause men to seek death. They will long to die, but death will flee from them (Rev. 9:6).

These locusts may truly be demonic in nature or they may be symbolic of troops in warfare. We find a parallel account of locusts recorded in the book of Joel. The prophet saw a vision of various types of locusts which would someday devastate the land of Israel. In Joel's vision, the locusts are identified as "a nation...mighty and without number" (Joel 1:6). Regarding this invading force, he wrote, "A day of darkness and gloom, a day of clouds and thick darkness. As the dawn is spread over the mountains, so there is a great and mighty people; there has never been anything like it, nor will there be again after it" (Joel 2:2). The locusts are also identified by God as "My great army" (Joel 2:25).

Additionally, when we compare the appearance of Joel's locusts to those in Revelation, they match identically. Both have teeth as the teeth of lions (Joel 1:6; Rev. 9:7), both make noise as the sound of many chariots (Joel 2:5; Rev. 9:9), both have the appearance of horses running to battle (Joel 2:4; Rev. 9:7, 9), and the locusts in Revelation have faces "like the faces of men" (Rev. 9:7), matching Joel's description of an invading human force.

With the War of Gog and Magog having begun shortly before the midpoint of the Tribulation, as revealed in the first four trumpets, it is likely the locusts of the fifth trumpet signify the continuation of this war involving Israel. Jesus warned, "When you see Jerusalem surrounded by armies, then recognize that her desolation is at hand" (Luke 21:20). He goes on to say, "Then let those who are in Judea flee to the mountains..." (Luke 21:21) He also warns that Israel should flee to the mountains of Judea when the Antichrist declares himself God (Matt. 24:15-21), which takes place at precisely the midpoint of the Tribulation when Satan is cast to the earth and physically indwells the body of the Antichrist.

At the sounding of the sixth trumpet, the second "woe" judgment, the 200-million-man army from the East heads to Israel as part of the campaign of Armageddon. Just as a quarter of the earth's population will perish within the fourth seal judgment, an additional one-third of mankind will perish by fire, smoke, and brimstone within this sixth trumpet judgment (Rev. 9:13-19).

The holocaust of the fifth and sixth trumpets sets the stage for the seven bowls of wrath, which clearly describe the effects of radioactivity on man and his environment as a result of a nuclear exchange.

The seventh trumpet, and final "woe" judgment, is placed in time at the end of the seven-year Tribulation after the seven bowls of wrath. Regarding this seventh trumpet, Scripture says, "And the nations were enraged, and Thy wrath came, and the time came for the dead to be judged, and the time to give their reward to Thy bondservants the prophets and to the saints and to those who fear Thy name, the small and the great, and to destroy those who destroy the earth" (Rev. 11:18).

With the sounding of the seventh trumpet, Jesus returns to earth to the battle of Armageddon to set up His millennial kingdom. But first, He must judge all who have survived the Tribulation, Jews and Gentiles alike. It is also at this time the Old Testament saints and all believers who died during the Tribulation face their day of judgment and reward.

Therefore, the seventh trumpet depicts the Second Advent Resurrection and Judgment Program at the conclusion of the Tribulation.

Remember, by this point, it is only the believers from the Day of Pentecost to the Rapture, when Jesus removes the Church, who will have already faced judgment. There, believers will stand at the Judgment Seat of Christ to receive their rewards for faithful service while the Tribulation is taking place on earth. Scripture is clear: Every knee shall bow and every tongue confess that "Jesus Christ is Lord, to the glory of God the Father" (Phil. 2:10-11). So every person to ever live will stand before Him in judgment at one point or another. This resurrection and judgment program will be discussed at length as we progress chronologically through the Tribulation.

The Bowls of Wrath

The seven bowls of wrath are recorded in Revelation 16. By this point in the Tribulation, God has sent the 144,000 Jewish witnesses to evangelize to the world of the coming of Christ, His two special messengers preaching repentance specifically to Israel, and the three angels flying in midheaven, the first of whom preaches an eternal gospel "to those who live on the earth, and to every nation and tribe and tongue and people" (Rev. 14:6). The third angel even exhorts the inhabitants of the earth not to receive the Mark of the Beast or else they will seal their eternal destiny in the lake of fire (Rev. 14:9-11).

But Scripture warns, "They made their hearts as an adamant stone, lest they should hear the law, and the words which the Lord of hosts hath sent in His Spirit by the former prophets; therefore came a great wrath from the Lord of hosts" (Zech. 7:12, KJV).

The bowls of wrath characterize the near destruction of mankind through the campaign of Armageddon. They depict the unrestrained fury of God upon a rebellious, sinful world at the end of the Great Tribulation. "Behold, the day of the Lord is coming, cruel, with fury and burning anger...I will punish the world for its evil, and the wicked for their iniquity...I will make mortal man scarcer than pure gold" (Isa. 13:9, 11, 12).

Again, as the seal judgments are an overview of the entire Tribulation, the bowls of wrath are incorporated within the sixth seal and also coincide with the fifth and sixth trumpets. In these bowls, we see the result of a nuclear holocaust which will involve all the nations of the world. Indeed, Scripture says, "I will gather all the nations against Jerusalem to battle" (Zech. 14:2).

Now, let's quickly summarize the world's population by the time the bowls of wrath are poured out. At the Rapture, which commences the Tribulation, perhaps as many as a billion people will vanish worldwide. I hope that figure is far surpassed, but based on the apostasy of the Laodicean church age in which we live, we must be conservative here. Then at the War of Gog and Magog shortly before the midpoint of the Tribulation, as much as 1.5 billion people may perish, and then countless millions will die during the worldwide persecution of Christians and Jews at the hands of the Antichrist during the Great Tribulation.

So at the conclusion of the Great Tribulation, maybe two billion or so will remain, and we know from the sixth trumpet, which coincides with the bowls of wrath, that one-third of them will perish during the fiery holocaust of Armageddon (Rev. 9:15; 9:18). Indeed, "Unless those days had been cut short, no life would have been saved" (Matt. 24:22). At this point, nearly all who remain will have accepted the Mark of the Beast, making them enemies of God, and He therefore "reserves wrath for His enemies" (Nah. 1:2).

The first bowl of wrath produces "loathsome and malignant sores" on all who accept the Mark of the Beast (Rev. 16:2). Though redemption is now too late for them, one would think after all that has taken place up to this point in the Tribulation, they would fall on their faces and beg forgiveness of Almighty God. Instead, Scripture says, "They gnawed their tongues because of pain, and they blasphemed the God of heaven because of their pains and their sores; and they did not repent of their deeds" (Rev. 16:11).

The second bowl is poured out on the sea, again a likely reference to the Mediterranean Sea, turning it to blood and killing every living thing therein. Likewise, the third bowl turns the rivers and springs of waters to blood. The reference to "blood" is symbolic of the contamination of these waters as a result of radioactivity. When we look back at the trumpets, Scripture says, "a great star fell from heaven, burning like a torch, and it fell on a third of the rivers and on the springs of waters; and the name of the star is called Wormwood...and many men died from the waters, because they were made bitter" (Rev. 8:10-11). Clearly, the "great star" depicts a nuclear missile, which indeed matches the description of a burning torch flying through the air. The name "Wormwood" is yet unclear and will only be revealed over time, but today, in the vast array of military arsenal, there are currently warheads known as "Silkworm" missiles. Therefore, the second and third bowls of wrath kill every living thing in the Mediterranean Sea and all who drink of the rivers and springs in that region (Rev. 16:6; cf. Rev. 17:6).

The fourth bowl causes the sun "to scorch men with fire" and "fierce heat." For those of us who live in the South, summers *do* feel like the fourth bowl of wrath, but even the hottest of our summers cannot compare to this extreme heat. The ozone layer, which surrounds the planet in the upper atmosphere, protects us from the harmful effects of the sun. If it were compressed and brought down to sea level, it would only be an eighth of an inch thick. When radioactivity is unleashed into the atmosphere, it will destroy this delicate, protective layer, causing the sun "to scorch men with fierce heat." Yet incredibly, "They blasphemed the name of God...and they did not repent, so as to give Him glory" (Rev. 16:9).

The fifth bowl of wrath is poured out "upon the throne of the beast," and, it says, "his kingdom became darkened" (Rev. 16:10). Here we see a darkening over Israel from the nuclear fallout of Armageddon. We know this is Israel because "the throne of the beast" depicts the throne in the Third Temple, which is to be built in Jerusalem by the midpoint of the Tribulation. The Antichrist, also known as the beast, will defile the temple by sitting on the throne and declaring himself God (2 Thess. 2:4).

The sixth bowl of wrath dries up the great Euphrates River, enabling the 200-million-man army from the East to successfully cross over (Rev. 16:12). This may be as a result of the intense, scorching heat of the fourth bowl of wrath, or it may be the result of man's intervention. Today, the Arab nation of Turkey controls the giant Ataturk Dam which regulates the flow of water into the Euphrates River. They may therefore assist the invading force from the East in their march through the desert and into the Holy Land.

Finally, the seventh bowl of wrath depicts demons going "out to the kings of the whole world to gather them together for the war of the great day of God, the Almighty" (Rev. 16:14). These demons are instrumental in leading all the nations of the world to converge on Israel "to the place which in Hebrew is called Har-Magedon" (Rev. 16:16), or Armageddon.

Chapter 7

The Tribulation

(Daniel's Seventieth Week)

The Tribulation will begin immediately following the Rapture. It is the final seven years of civilization as we know it. To better understand this, we must defer to the prophet Daniel, who recorded Israel's future through a period of seventy "weeks" of years (Dan. 9:24-27).

In 538 B.C., while in Babylonian captivity, Daniel read Jeremiah's prophecy of Israel's captivity in Babylon lasting for seventy years. He also discovered that afterward, the Jews would return to their homeland (Jer. 25:11; 29:10). Daniel realized sixty-seven of the seventy years had already passed, and he began a lengthy intercessory prayer for the restoration and deliverance of the Jews from their captivity.

While he was praying, the Lord sent the angel Gabriel to reveal to Daniel the future of the Jewish people. Gabriel announced, "Seventy weeks have been decreed for your people and your holy city, to finish the transgression, to make an end of sin, to make atonement for iniquity, to bring in everlasting righteousness, to seal up vision and prophecy, and to anoint the most holy place" (Dan. 9:24). In this passage, the Hebrew word for "weeks" is "shabua," meaning "seven." Therefore, the total time of "seventy weeks" for Israel's future would be 490 years, or seventy times seven. Gabriel goes on to say the seventy weeks would be borne out in three segments of time, which would begin immediately upon the decree to restore and rebuild Jerusalem (Dan. 9:25-26).

The first time period given is seven weeks, or forty-nine years. In 445 B.C., nearly a hundred years after Gabriel revealed Israel's future events to Daniel, Artaxerxes Longimanus issued the decree to restore and rebuild Jerusalem (Neh. 2:4-8). This marked the point at which Israel's seventy weeks, or 490 years, would begin to count down.

The second time period given is sixty-two weeks, or 434 years. This period began at the conclusion of the first period and ended on Palm Sunday when the Lord Jesus rode into Jerusalem on a donkey. He was rejected by the Jews as their King and Messiah and crucified that following Friday. Even as Jesus approached Jerusalem, He knew He would be rejected. He prophesied of His rejection in a parable of the nobleman who was leaving to a distant country to receive his kingdom. The nobleman is symbolic of Jesus. "But his citizens hated him, and sent a delegation after him, saying, 'We do not want this man to reign over us'" (Luke 19:14). The Jews were expecting their King to be a mighty conquerer, not a lowly carpenter. They failed to see the coming of the Messiah first, as sacrifice, then as conquering King.

So we have the first period of seven weeks and the second period of sixty-two weeks, bringing the total time of Israel's history to sixty-nine weeks, or 483 years. However, when the Lord Jesus was rejected by the Jews, Israel's prophetic time clock abruptly stopped, with seven years remaining to complete Gabriel's prophecy of 490 years. God then gave the Jews "a spirit of stupor, eyes to see not and ears to hear not" (Rom. 11:8). The apostle Paul wrote, "A partial hardening has happened to Israel until the fulness of the Gentiles has come in" (Rom. 11:25). The Jews were the chosen of God to bring the message of salvation to the whole world, but when they rejected their Messiah, God directed His attention to the Gentiles to bring the message of salvation, and thus began the Church Age. For nearly 2,000 years, the Church has been the focus of God's redemptive activity. Just as Israel's prophetic time clock stopped at the birth of the Church, the removal of the Church at the Rapture will resume it. At that point, God will then redirect His focus to the Jews for the remaining seven years of Gabriel's prophecy, or Daniel's Seventieth Week.

Contrary to popular belief, the Tribulation is not a period of time set aside for God to vent His anger on mankind for His thousands of years of suppressed anger due to our sin and rebellion. Some parents might do so under the same circumstances, but our loving and patient Father is not like that. This will be the worst time in human history, but not because God is "getting even" with man.

While God will purge the earth of sin during the Tribulation and judge its political and religious systems, its primary purpose is to prepare the Jews for the Messiah who is coming to fulfill God's Word. Jesus will return to earth at the end of the Tribulation to establish His millennial reign in fulfillment of three covenants made by God for the nation of Israel. Though the earth and nearly all of its inhabitants will be destroyed, a remnant of *Jews and Gentiles* will enter the Millennium in their physical bodies as the recipients of God's unconditional promises made to Abraham and his seed thousands of years ago. Paul wrote, "There is neither Jew nor Greek, there is neither slave nor free man, there is neither male nor female; for you are all one in Christ Jesus. And if you belong to Christ, then you are Abraham's offspring, heirs according to promise" (Gal. 3:28-29). So Gentiles are also recipients of the covenants promised to Abraham, but events of the Tribulation will be centered around the Jews and the nation of Israel.

God made three unconditional covenants with Israel which have not been fulfilled. Their fulfillment is mandatory based on the character and integrity of God. God is incapable of untruths or broken promises, and when He makes a covenant, it will absolutely be fulfilled. "My covenant I will not violate, nor will I alter the utterance of My lips" (Ps. 89:34). Thus the preparatory seven-year Tribulation is primarily to usher in the millennial reign of Christ in fulfillment of God's covenants to His people.

The first of three yet-to-be-fulfilled covenants is found in the book of Genesis. There we find the Abrahamic covenant where God promised Abraham his descendants would occupy all the land of Canaan. God told him, "All the land which you see, I will give it to you and to your descendants forever" (Gen. 13:15). God also promised him the number of his descendants would be "as the stars of the heavens, and as the sand which is on the seashore" (Gen. 22:17). Additionally, God promised in Abraham's seed "all the families of the earth shall be blessed," that his descendants will be "as the dust of the earth; so that if anyone can number the dust of the earth, then (his) descendants can also be numbered" (Gen. 12:3; 13:16). This covenant will be fulfilled during Christ's millennial reign on earth.

The second yet-to-be-fulfilled promise of God is the Palestinic covenant, as recorded in the book of Deuteronomy. Through this covenant, God promised that Israel would fully repent, that all would be converted, and that the Lord would return and restore them to their land (Deut. 30:1-10). It also provides the basis upon which the land of Canaan will someday be occupied by Abraham's descendants.

Finally, the third yet-to-be-fulfilled promise of God is the Davidic covenant, as recorded in the books of 2 Samuel, Jeremiah, and the Psalms. In the Davidic covenant, God promised David a son who would be a king; Solomon. But God also promised in David's seed an eternal throne and an everlasting kingdom would be established, that of the Lord Jesus'.

Though the horrors of the Tribulation focus on the nation of Israel, God assures them, "Just as I brought all this great disaster on this people, so I am going to bring on them all the good that I am promising them" (Jer. 32:42). Christ's millennial kingdom will fulfill all the covenants He has made with His people. The secondary purpose for the Tribulation is *then* to purge the earth of sin and rebellion.

The Tribulation must be seen in three sections: the first half, the midpoint, and the second half. Each half totals forty-two months, with each month lasting thirty days. Therefore, each half contains exactly 1,260 days, or 3½ years, with the two halves totaling seven years. At the midpoint, a pivotal event takes place commencing the second half of the Tribulation, what is referred to as the Great Tribulation. It will be a perilous time, to which the prophet Jeremiah referred as like unto "the time of Jacob's trouble" (Jer. 30:7, KJV), indeed one in which Jesus warned "has not occurred since the beginning of the world until now, nor ever shall" (Matt. 24:21).

The Oslo Peace Accord

On September 13, 1993, after two years of U.S.-brokered negotiations, the late Israeli prime minister Yitzhak Rabin, PLO leader Yasser Arafat, and U.S. president Bill Clinton shook hands in agreement over what were then acceptable peace terms between the history-long rivals. Among its declarations, the Oslo Peace Accord stipulated Israel would trade six major towns in the West Bank, including Jericho, to the Palestinians in exchange for peace.

Politicians applauded and people the world over celebrated, but many in Israel did not. They viewed the agreement as the Palestinians taking one step closer to making good on their threats to wipe them out. In fact, Yasser Arafat once said, "Peace for us means the destruction of Israel." So his signature across a document meant nothing to them. Clearly, the less land Israel has, the more vulnerable they are to attack.

This fact did not go unnoticed by one Jewish student named Yigal Amir. On November 4, 1995, ironically the night Yitzhak Rabin was attending a peace rally in Tel Aviv, the young student opened fire on the prime minister, killing him. Rabin had previously signed a peace accord with the late King Hussein of Jordan in October of 1994 and was in negotiation with Syrian president Hafez Assad over trading the Golan Heights for peace, the strategic mountainous territory located between Northern Israel and Syria. Rabin's death halted the process, but not Syria's desire for the land. The Jerusalem Post in August of 1997 quoted Syrian chief of staff Hikhmat Shihabi as saying they would "take back the Golan Heights by force if it cannot do so peacefully." Without the Heights, Israel would be defenseless against an invading foe from the north. Notwithstanding, they will likely relinquish this territory since Scripture warns of an invading force from the north coming against the mountains of Israel (Ezek. 39:2).

The assassination of Yitzhak Rabin was critical to end-time events. Rabin mistakenly believed that by trading land for peace, Israel would somehow satisfy her Arab neighbors. But the Arabs are committed, even to the point of death, to the eradication of the Jews in the Middle East. In so doing, the Arabs are fulfilling an ordinance of the Muslim faith and thereby pleasing Allah, their god. In the prophetical scheme of things, Rabin had to die to prepare the way for Israel's next prime minister, Benjamin Netanyahu, a man faithfully devoted to seeing the Jews retain the territory promised them by God.

The terms of the Oslo Peace Accord expired on May 4, 1999, but an agreement was reached to extend its terms for a short time. Once they expire, whatever was initially agreed upon in September of 1993 will become null and void. If the accord is not fully implemented by the time of its deadline, Palestinian leader Yasser Arafat has promised to unilaterally declare the West Bank a Palestinian state, making Jerusalem its capital.

Because of violence and constant terrorist attacks, the peace process stalled for 19 months, but realizing the urgency of the impending deadline, the Middle East leaders reconvened in October of 1998 at the Wye River Plantation in Maryland in an attempt to resume the peace process. After nine days of intense negotiation, an agreement was finally reached on October 23, 1998, in what is now referred to as the Wye Accord. The terms of this treaty revolve around implementation of the Oslo Accord.

Once again, the world applauded as efforts for peace in the Mideast seemed underway, but the accord has proven to be disastrous, with problem upon problem and little being done to resume the process at all. Netanyahu's agreement to cede an additional 13% of the West Bank to the Palestinians came as a surprise to even his most staunch supporters. Living among 1.5 million Palestinians, the 150,000 Israeli settlers in the West Bank felt their leader betrayed them, and they stood resistant to the accord, staging continual protests. As well, hardliners within the Israeli and Palestinian cabinets rejected the accord, prompting U.S. negotiators to feverishly work toward resolving the issues before the May 4, 1999, expiration of the Oslo Accord.

The European Union's absence in the Wye Accord peace talks hardly went unnoticed. In May of 1998, the EU hosted a peace summit in London for the Middle East leaders, acting as the Palestinians' representative, while the U.S. acted on behalf of Israel. In April of 1998, one month prior to the London summit, Yasser Arafat stated at a press conference, "Our position has always been that the European Union must have a vital, effective role in this peace process." Yet in the Wye River Plantation meeting held only five months later, the EU was nowhere to be found. The terms of the Wye Accord established a land-for-security deal in which Israel demands a guarantee of security from Palestinians against terrorist attacks before they will relinquish territory in the West Bank. But so far, the agreement has proven to be something the Palestinians cannot enforce, and the situation continues to escalate.

Indeed, the EU will prove to have a vital role in the peace process, acting on behalf of the Palestinians to guarantee Israel's security. A man is about to emerge from within the EU who will have the perfect solution, giving the Arabs the land they want, yet promising Israel the peace she so desperately seeks. Richard Nixon once said, "The greatest honor history can bestow is that of a peacemaker." According to the Scriptures, a peacemaker is definitely on the horizon, but hardly one in whom honor can be bestowed.

So What About the United States?

As we begin to study events in the Tribulation, it must be pointed out that Scripture is strangely silent about the West. Speculation abounds as to why, but a plausible explanation may be found in the Y2K bug, which may well bring the United States to its knees. Our nation rests heavily on computers written in an antiquated language which cannot conform to the 00 numbers of the new century without first rewriting extensive lines of computer language. While the problem has been given top priority, there is literally not enough time remaining to rewrite the millions of lines of code needed to operate the computer systems of governmental agencies, banks, utility companies, the transportational system, including planes, trains, and ships, which permit the importing and exporting of goods into and out of this country, as well as the nation's defense system, to name a few. This crisis may paralyze the United States and serve as a reason for its absence in the Scriptures. How long its effect may last, only time will tell.

The First 3½ Years

> *Anyone who relies on outside security will be committing suicide.*
>
> David Bar Illam
> Senior Policy Adviser to
> Former Israeli Prime Minister
> Benjamin Netanyahu
> CNN World News
> May 14, 1998

The Tribulation begins following the Rapture of the Church. Immediately, 144,000 Jews throughout the world will accept Christ and begin evangelizing, telling of His imminent return and the need for repentance. The conversion of these Jews will likely stem from a supernatural event, much like the apostle Paul's conversion to Christianity while on the road to Damascus (Acts 9). As well, God's Two Witnesses will begin their ministry in Israel for exactly 1,260 days, or the entirety of the first half of the Tribulation. These two men will come in judgment, causing drought, famine, and plagues on the earth, yet unceasingly preaching repentance. They will be hated by the world because of the torment they inflict (Rev. 11). On the political scene, Israel will secure her long-awaited peace, while a false religious figure known as the False Prophet will surface to exalt the man who made it happen.

As well, an apostate religious system known as "the great harlot" will begin to emerge. This includes the professing church, those who claimed to be saved when they were not and, as such, were left behind at the Rapture. These are the ones of which Jesus spoke when He said, "'Not everyone who says to Me, 'Lord, Lord,' will enter the kingdom of heaven; but he who does the will of My Father who is in heaven. Many will say to Me on that day, 'Lord, Lord, did we not prophesy in Your name, and in Your name cast out demons, and in Your name perform many miracles?' And then I will declare to them, 'I never knew you; depart from Me, you who practice lawlessness'" (Matt. 7:21-23).

At the outset of the Tribulation, the crisis in the Middle East over the Oslo Peace Accord will immediately be resolved by a man emerging out of Europe, the Antichrist. Scripture says, "He shall confirm the covenant with many for one week...." (Dan. 9:27, KJV, emphasis mine) The word "confirm" means to "ratify," "strengthen," or "make firm," which necessarily denotes a covenant, or agreement, which has already been established. He will simply uphold the terms and conditions of a preceding treaty, those of the Oslo Peace Accord. The reference to "week" is to Daniel's Seventieth Week, the Tribulation.

As leader of a member nation in the European Union, the Antichrist will somehow convince Israel that their security can rest in this powerful bloc of nations to protect them. After all, the European Union currently includes fifteen member nations, totaling nearly half a billion people, and boasts of a combined gross domestic product of $6.5 trillion, making them the most powerful economic force in the world. Presumably then, if the EU, as the Palestinians' representative, guarantees Israel's security, they will feel confident to let down their guard.

In fact, that is exactly what they will do. Israel will agree to the terms of the covenant confirmed by the Antichrist. His promise of guaranteed peace will lull them into a false sense of security, for they are seen living in a "land of unwalled villages," people "who are at rest, that live securely, all of them living without walls, and having no bars or gates" (Ezek. 38:11).

Their peaceful occupation will be shortlived, however. Like *everything* out of Satan's mouth, the promise will be a lie, a false covenant. The prophet Isaiah wrote of this, stating, "We have made a covenant with death, and with Sheol we have made a pact" (Isa. 28:15a). He goes on to say, "We have made falsehood our refuge and we have concealed ourselves with deception" (Isa. 28:15b). Jeremiah wrote of this same covenant, "They have healed the brokenness of My people superficially, saying, 'Peace, peace,' but there is no peace" (Jer. 6:14). The Antichrist, through the European Union, will guarantee Israel's security, enabling them to live in peace, but he will betray the Jews by breaking the treaty 3½ years later (Dan. 9:27).

The Revived Roman Empire

Over 2500 years ago, Nebuchadnezzar, king of Babylon, had a troubling dream. When he awoke, he had forgotten what the dream was, yet he wanted an explanation. He summoned magicians, conjurers, sorcerers, and astrologers to, first, tell him the dream, and then interpret its meaning. Of course, no one was able. So he ordered all the wise men of Babylon killed, including the prophet Daniel, who was being held in the Babylonian captivity. When Daniel found out what was going on, he asked to interpret the dream for the king, and permission was granted. God then revealed the dream to

Daniel in a vision (Dan. 2).

Nebuchadnezzar had seen into the future. He saw a great statue standing in front of him with a head of fine gold, its chest and arms of silver, its belly and thighs of bronze, its legs of iron, with the feet and toes partly of iron and clay. In the interpretation of the dream, the statue represented four kingdoms or empires which would rule successively over the entire earth. The head of gold represented the mighty Babylonian Empire with Nebuchadnezzar as king. The chest and arms of silver represented the Medo-Persian Empire under Darius and Cyrus the Persian. The belly and thighs of bronze represented the Grecian Empire under Alexander the Great. And, lastly, the legs of iron, along with the feet and toes partly of iron and clay, represented the fourth world-ruling kingdom, the mighty Roman Empire (Dan. 2).

Later, the prophet Daniel saw a vision which paralleled Nebuchadnezzar's dream of four world-ruling empires. However, in Daniel's vision, the empires are characterized by four voracious beasts (Dan. 7). The first three beasts are described as a lion with eagle's wings, a bear with its paw raised and three ribs in its mouth, and a four-headed leopard with wings of a fowl on its back. Yet the fourth beast is described differently. It is depicted as exceedingly dreadful, extremely strong, terrifying, having large iron teeth and claws of bronze. The beast had ten horns with an additional "little horn" coming up from among them. The "little horn" is described as having "eyes like the eyes of a man, and a mouth uttering great boasts" (Dan. 7:8).

Daniel sought the meaning of the vision. He was told, "These great beasts, which are four in number, are four kings who will arise from the earth" (Dan. 7:17). But he was particularly disturbed by the fourth beast and wanted to know the exact meaning of it. He was told, "The fourth beast will be a fourth kingdom on the earth, which will be different from all the other kingdoms, and it will devour the whole earth and tread it down and crush it. As for the ten horns, out of this kingdom ten kings will arise; and another will arise after them, and he will be different from the previous ones and will subdue three kings" (Dan. 7:23-24).

As sure as it is written in God's Word, it will come to pass. As a matter of fact, the phrase "come (or came) to pass" is mentioned in the Scriptures more than 600 times. From Daniel's vision onward, history records the four world-ruling kingdoms began with the Babylonian Empire, spanning from 605 B.C. to 539 B.C.; the Medo-Persian Empire, from 539 B.C. to 331 B.C.; the Grecian Empire, from 331 B.C. to 242 B.C.; and finally the Roman Empire, which initially conquered Sicily in 242 B.C., and subsequently the remainder of the Mediterranean world. The Roman Empire, however, was never conquered by an invading force. As the centuries passed, the power and glory of the fourth world-ruling empire simply diminished. Finally, in 476 A.D., Rome fell, only existing thereafter as a religious empire.

But Daniel recorded ten kings as part of the fourth and final world-ruling empire, as does the book of Revelation. "The ten horns which you saw are ten kings, who have not yet received a kingdom, but they receive authority as kings with the beast for one hour. These have one purpose and they give their power and authority to the beast" (Rev. 17:12-13). Ten kings have never ruled simultaneously within the ancient Roman Empire. It must therefore necessitate a *revived* formation, characterized by an alliance of ten nations.

Most students of prophecy agree that the powerful European Union represents the revived Roman Empire. Without question, it is *the* foremost economic bloc in the world. However, the EU currently has fifteen member nations with dozens slated to follow, leaving us to speculate on a reformation of the European Union. But Daniel wrote, *"Out of this kingdom* ten kings will arise" (Dan. 7:24, italics mine). In other words, out of the European Union as the revived Roman Empire, ten kings will arise.

So much focus has been on the European Union that few have noticed the ten-nation alliance of the Western European Union. In fact, the WEU is the *defense* arm of the European Union and the division through which guarantees of security can be made. The Maastricht Declarations established in December 1991, state: "The Western European Union will be developed as the defense component of the European Union and as the means to strengthen the European pillar of the Atlantic Alliance. To this end, it will formulate a common European defense policy and carry forward its concrete implementation through the further development of its own operational role."

So at the outset of the Tribulation, a man will arise out of the ten-nation Western European Union, the defense arm of the powerful EU. He will confirm the Oslo Peace Accord, giving the Palestinians the land they want, while guaranteeing Israel their security. As such, for nearly 3½ years after the Tribulation begins, with the Arab/Israeli conflict seemingly resolved, the world will experience relative peace, yet at the same time suffer terribly through drought, famine, and plagues wrought by God's Two Witnesses, whose ministry of judgment lasts until the midpoint. All the while, the 144,000 Jewish evangelists will faithfully proclaim the name of Jesus, turning the hearts of countless millions to Christ. It is also within this time that a false religious figure will emerge, the

False Prophet, who will perform many miraculous signs and point the way to the Antichrist as God. As well, the apostate church known as the "great harlot" will emerge.

The Third Jewish Temple

After the Rapture of the Church and by the midpoint of the Tribulation, the Third Jewish Temple will be built in Jerusalem (Dan. 9:27; Zech. 1:14-16; 2 Thess. 2:4; Rev. 11:1-2). No doubt the Antichrist's influence over the Palestinians will make this a possibility. According to Jewish law, the Temple must be built on the original site of Solomon's Temple. Known as the Temple Mount, this 35-acre tract of land is undoubtedly the most volatile piece of property in the world. Not only is the Third Jewish Temple to be built there, but it currently houses two of Islam's holiest shrines, the Al Aqsa Mosque and the Dome of the Rock, which presents a major problem between the two faiths.

In late 1990, the Temple Mount Faithful, a Jewish group dedicated to the construction of the Temple, actually attempted to begin construction by laying its four-ton cornerstone. This enraged the Palestinians and a riot ensued thereafter in which seventeen people were killed. Once again, in October of 1998, the Temple Mount Faithful set out to lay the cornerstone. This time the hopeful group was stopped by angry Palestinians without violence. Needless to say, the Antichrist must be instrumental in controlling the peace and allowing this event to take place.

The First Jewish Temple was built by King Solomon. It was known for its lavish beauty more than its great size. It was destroyed in 586 B.C. when the Babylonians under King

Nebuchadnezzar burned Jerusalem. Later, under Zerubbabel, Jewish exiles of the Babylonian captivity returned to their homeland and built the Second Temple, completing its modest structure in 516 B.C.

Nearly 500 years later, in 20 B.C., Herod the Great began a massive renovation of the Temple. A tireless builder, his decision to renovate was motivated only by the desire to bring prestige unto himself. However, he died before its completion, and in 64 A.D., under King Herod Agrippa II, the brilliant 26-acre, white marble structure was fully completed, 84 years after construction initially began. Six years later, in 70 A.D., all but the western wall of the Temple was totally destroyed when the Roman general Titus conquered Jerusalem. We know it today as the Wailing Wall where Orthodox Jews gather to pray for the Temple's restoration.

In anticipation of the construction of the Temple, preparation for Temple worship has long been underway. For nearly twenty years, rabbis at the Temple Institute in Jerusalem have been preparing Jewish students from the priestly tribe of Levi in the knowledge and fulfillment of their duties once the Temple is completed. Over 80 objects and utensils, including musical instruments of the Bible, have currently been replicated for Temple service.

Of much significance to the rebuilding of the Temple and the resumption of Temple worship is the search for the perfect red heifer. In Numbers chapter 19, an ordinance was established by God for the purification of sin before entry into the Temple. A perfect, unblemished red heifer is to be sacrificed and its ashes mixed with spring water to cleanse the high priest from sin.

In June of 1997, CNN reported the perfect red heifer had been born on a farm in Northern Israel. Dubbed "Melody," the red heifer instigated a swarm of controversy between Jews and Arabs and ignited apocalyptic fervor the world over. Arabs feared the discovery would signal the construction of the Third Temple. But despite all the excitement, in January of 1998, it was determined that Melody had failed the test of perfection when her owner discovered white hairs on her tail, rendering her an unacceptable sacrifice.

Famed archaeologist Vendyl Jones believes the ashes of the red heifer lie in a cave north of Qumran, the cave in which the Dead Sea Scrolls were discovered in 1947. Qumran is also near a spring of fresh water known as Ain Feshkha. Jones has been digging for the ashes since 1977.

Along with the ashes of the perfect red heifer, there are two other essential components to the resumption of Temple worship; the oil and the incense (Ex. 30:22-38). The holy oil must be of precise ingredients as established by God. It was used to anoint the priests for service, as well as the Temple structure with its many utensils and furnishings. The incense must also be of precise ingredients as established by God.

Incredibly, in 1988, Vendyl Jones and his excavating team unearthed a container of oil which, upon further examination, matched the ingredients of the holy anointing oil needed for Temple worship. Later, in May of 1992, they discovered a trough containing a red substance which also matched the ingredients of the incense.

Though it would be a thrilling discovery to find the Ark of the Covenant, it is not required to resume Temple worship. It was certainly not present at the Second Temple, which the Jews built after returning from Babylonian captivity. In fact, the Ark has been missing for nearly 3,000 years, and its location still remains a mystery. But recent word out of Israel is that Vendyl Jones may be close to discovering its whereabouts as well.

When the Jews recaptured Jerusalem in the Six-Day War of 1967, the event which marked the "budding of the fig tree," Jewish historian, Israel Eldad, made this incredible statement: "We are at the stage at which David was when he liberated Jerusalem. From that time until the construction of the Temple by Solomon, only one generation passed. So will it be with us."[1]

Clearly, the Third Jewish Temple will be built *by* the midpoint of the Tribulation, for there will be the cessation of Temple worship rituals at that time. "And he will make a firm covenant with the many for one week, but in the middle of the week he will put a stop to sacrifice and grain offering...." (Dan. 9:27).

The War of Gog and Magog

Nearly 2600 years ago, the prophet Ezekiel warned of a mighty military force that would someday invade Israel (see Ezek. 38-39). This invasion is referred to as the War of Gog and Magog, and it begins shortly before the midpoint of the Tribulation. It is the first in a series of battles that will extend over the entire second half of the Tribulation. In the book of Revelation, the battle of Armageddon is referred to as "the battle of that great day of God Almighty" (Rev. 16:14, KJV). The Greek word used for "battle" in this passage is "polemos," meaning "war" or "campaign," while "mache" signifies "a battle," and in certain cases single combat. The War of Gog and Magog begins the campaign of warfare, culminating with the battle of Armageddon at the end of the Tribulation.[2]

During the War of Gog and Magog, three movements

into Palestine will occur. Scripture warns, "At the end time the king of the South will collide with him, and the king of the North will storm against him..." (Dan. 11:40). Shortly before the midpoint of the Tribulation, an invading force will enter Israel from the south. Because the Antichrist, through a federation of ten nations, has promised to protect Israel, he and his forces will then move into Palestine. While this is taking place, an alliance of nations will then invade Israel from the north. Remember, this campaign will begin shortly before the midpoint of the Tribulation. By this point, the Antichrist has not yet ascended to world ruler. He is still the leader of a single European nation.

The King of the South

Throughout Scripture, Egypt is commonly referred to as the land of the South. Egypt will likely make the first move in the war, sending its forces into Israel to attack Jerusalem.

The Antichrist and His Army

Because the Antichrist has promised to protect Israel through his ten-nation federation, when the Egyptian forces invade Israel, he will come to her defense and move his army into Palestine.

Incredibly, in October of 1998, British Prime Minister Tony Blair announced plans for developing a European Union army within NATO, one in which joint military operations would be permitted between member nations of the EU and facilitated through the Western European Union, the defense arm of the EU as established under the terms of the Maastricht Treaty. Blair cited a need for the EU to have its own military "identity," allowing them to stage and oversee peacekeeping missions in Europe without having to consult other members of NATO. The United States has given its approval to the plan.

The King of the North

At about the same time, an assembly of nations will invade Israel from the north. Because this massive force enters Israel from the north, the entire alliance is referred to as the Northern Confederacy or the Northern Alliance. Scripture warns, "You will come from your place out of the remote parts of the north, you and many peoples with you...a great assembly and a mighty army; and you will come up against My people Israel like a cloud to cover the land" (Ezek. 38:15-16). The leader of the Northern Confederacy is referred to as Gog, the King of the North. He is not the Antichrist. They are two different individuals.

Gog is the chief prince of Rosh, Meshech, and Tubal from the land of Magog (Ezek. 38:2-3). Magog was the name of the second son of Japheth, who was the oldest son of Noah. Magog's descendants, the Scythians, inhabited the land north of the Black and Caspian Seas, now modern-day Russia. Meshech and Tubal were also names of Japheth's sons. Meshech speaks of Moscow, the capital of Russia, and Tubal of Tobolsk, the earliest province of Asiatic Russia to be colonized, while Rosh is believed to be another name for Russia.[3] When Gog invades Israel, he will bring all but a sixth of Russia with him in the invasion (Ezek. 39:2, KJV). Therefore, Russia will be the predominant force in the Northern Confederacy. At this very moment, events in Russia warn of the likely imminent return to militant Communism.

A number of Arab and African nations will join Russia in this invasion into Palestine. The first alliance with Gog will be Persia (Ezek. 38:5), which is modern-day Iran. The second alliance will be Ethiopia (Ezek. 38:5). While the reference is apparent to the East-African nation, there are eleven references in Scripture to Ethiopia as the land of Cush, which denotes at least a portion of Arabia. The third alliance with Gog will be Put (Ezek. 38:5). Its geographical location is widely accepted as the modern African nation of Libya. The fourth allied nation will be Gomer (Ezek. 38:6). Gomer was the name of another of Japheth's sons whose descendants were the Cimmerians occupying central Turkey during the Assyrian Empire. The reference to Gomer therefore likely depicts the nation of Turkey. The fifth Russian alliance will be Beth-togarmah (Ezek. 38:6). Togarmah was Japheth's grandson, the third son of Gomer. These descendants settled in the territory generally accepted as Armenia and may include certain Asiatic countries as well.[4] Finally, "many peoples" (Ezek. 38:6, 15) will also align with this Northern bloc of nations, but who they are remains to be seen.

For nearly 3½ years into the Tribulation, the Jews will live securely in their own land by virtue of the Antichrist's guarantee of security. As leader of the ten-nation European alliance, the Antichrist will confirm a covenant with Israel, promising to protect the Jews from hostile Arab nations through the use of his own security forces. As such, Israel will be lulled into a false sense of security, not standing ready in her own defense. They are seen "at rest, living securely...without walls and having no bars or gates" (Ezek. 38:11). Gog will consider them easy prey, and he and his alliance will therefore invade Israel from the north to "seize plunder, to carry away silver and gold, to take away cattle and goods, to capture great spoil" (Ezek. 38:13, 15).

The Outcome of the War

When the Egyptian forces enter Israel, the Antichrist and his army will move into Palestine to defend Israel. They will move downward into Egypt and collide with the advancing Egyptian army. At that point, Scripture says, "He will gain control over the hidden treasures of gold and silver, and over all the precious things of Egypt" (Dan. 11:43). The Antichrist and his forces will be victorious in the confrontation. "But rumors from the East and from the North will disturb him, and he will go forth with great wrath to destroy and annihilate many. And he will pitch the tents of his royal pavilion between the seas and the Holy Mountain" (Dan. 11:44-45). While they are subduing the Egyptian army, the Russian alliance will invade Israel from the north. The Antichrist and his forces will then make their headquarters in Jerusalem and prepare to go against the Northern Confederacy, but this time the Lord God will intervene on Israel's behalf.

Gog and his mighty military force will not prevail against Israel. Scripture says, "'It will come about on that day, when Gog comes against the land of Israel,' declares the Lord God, 'that My fury will mount up in My anger. And in My zeal and in My blazing wrath I declare that on that day there will surely be a great earthquake in the land of Israel. And I shall call for a sword against him on all My mountains,' declares the Lord God. 'Every man's sword will be against his brother. And with pestilence and with blood I shall enter into judgment with him; and I shall rain on him, and on his troops, and on the many peoples who are with him, a torrential rain, with hailstones, fire, and brimstone'" (Ezek. 38:18-19).

When Gog and his alliance invade Israel, Almighty God will fight against them using the forces of nature, combined with man-made weapons of destruction. In a parallel passage, Scripture says, "The Lord will cause His voice of authority to be heard. And the descending of His arm to be seen in fierce anger, and in the flame of a consuming fire, in cloudburst, downpour, and hailstones...and in battles, brandishing weapons, He will fight them" (Isa. 30:30, 32).

In another passage, Scripture says, "I will make a violent wind break out in My wrath. There will also be in My anger a flooding rain and hailstones to consume it in wrath" (Ezek. 13:13). Again, "Upon the wicked He will rain snares; fire and brimstone and burning wind will be the portion of their cup" (Ps. 11:6).

That the invading force will perish by the sword is a clear indication of conventional warfare. Pestilence probably indicates biological warfare. Fire, brimstone, and burning wind are all components of nuclear activity. In fact, brimstone is actually sulphur and a component of chemical weapons. The torrential rains and hailstones will likely stem from a disruption of the atmosphere related to the intrusion of nuclear activity. During a nuclear explosion, the force of the blast compresses the atmosphere, pushing it into the upper layers of the stratosphere where the humid air is frozen and falls back to the earth in the form of giant hailstones. This will surely account for the 100-pound hailstones that will fall at Armageddon (Rev. 16:21).

Gog and his Northern Confederacy will be killed on the Golan Heights, the northern mountains of Israel. "You shall fall on the mountains of Israel, you and all your troops, and the peoples who are with you; I shall give you as food to every kind of predatory bird and beast of the field" (Ezek.

39:4). They "will eat until they are glutted" (Ezek. 39:17-20). As many as 1.5 billion people may die in the conflict. It will take all of Israel seven months to bury the dead and seven years to dispose of the debris. They will be buried in what will be called the Valley of Hamon-gog, which means "the multitude of Gog" (Ezek. 39:9-12).

God will intervene on Israel's behalf to bring glory unto Himself. Scripture says, "I shall set My glory among the nations; and all the nations will see My judgment which I have executed, and My hand which I have laid on them. And the house of Israel will know that I am the Lord their God from that day onward" (Ezek. 39:21-22). Yet despite the miraculous, the nations of the world will give the glory to the Antichrist. Gog's defeat will be attributed to the Antichrist's army moving against him, combined with the forces of nature.

This war will undoubtedly create world chaos and promote more of the New World Order propaganda, underscoring the need for a one-world government. Since the Antichrist upheld his promise to defend Israel in the name of peace, he will be perceived as a man of integrity and trustworthiness. From within his ten-nation federation, he will rapidly ascend in worldwide power. Regarding these ten nations, Scripture says, "These have one purpose and they give their power and authority to the beast" (Rev. 17:13).

Former Secretary General of NATO, Paul Henri Spaak, once said, "We do not want another committee; we have too many already. What we want is a man of sufficient stature to hold the allegiance of all people and to lift us out of the economic morass into which we are sinking. Send us such a man and be he god or devil, we will receive him."[5]

After all the conflict has ended, the Antichrist and his troops will continue to stay in Jerusalem, supposedly for her protection. By the midpoint of the Tribulation, he will be elevated to world ruler. Scripture says, "And the whole earth was amazed and followed after the beast...and they worshiped the beast, saying, 'Who is like the beast, and who is able to wage war with him?'" (Rev. 13:3-4). He will remain in power as *world* ruler for the remainder of the Tribulation. "Authority to act for forty-two months was given to him...and authority over every tribe and people and tongue and nation was given to him" (Rev. 13:5, 7).

The Great Harlot is Destroyed

For the first half of the Tribulation, this apostate religious system will permeate and influence the world (Rev. 17:2). It is described as "Babylon the Great, the Mother of Harlots and of the Abominations of the Earth" (Rev. 17:5) because it characterizes the false religions which prevailed during the Babylonian era. This harlot religious system will threaten the agenda of the False Prophet, who has been pointing the way to the Antichrist as God. The ten nations and the beast will "hate the harlot" and destroy her (Rev. 17:16) in order for the Antichrist to be the sole object of worship during the latter half of the Tribulation.

The Midpoint

> *Keep on the alert at all times, praying in order that you may have strength to escape all these things that are about to take place, and to stand before the Son of Man.*
>
> Luke 21:36

Everything takes a drastic turn at this pivotal point in the Tribulation. A number of critical events will occur at this time. Initially, a seal will be supernaturally placed on the foreheads of the 144,000 Jewish evangelists to protect them from the horrors of the second half of the Tribulation (Rev. 7:1-8). As well, the three angels flying in midheaven will begin proclaiming their successive messages to the entire world (Rev. 14:6-11).

The Abomination of Desolation

Up to this point in the Tribulation, Satan has controlled the movements of the Antichrist and False Prophet. However, at precisely the midpoint, he will physically indwell the body of the Antichrist. Scripture warns, "Woe to the earth and the sea, because the devil has come down to you, having great wrath, knowing that he has only a short time" (Rev. 12:12). As a result, the last half of the Tribulation "will be a time of distress such as never occurred since there was a nation until that time" (Dan. 12:1). Only 3½ years will remain until Jesus comes back to earth.

Satan has always wanted to be God, but the most he will ever be is a pathetic fallen angel. In his five "I wills" (Isa. 14:13-14), he vowed "to raise (his) throne above the stars of God...and make (himself) like the Most High," but as Beelzebub, he has ascended only as high as "lord of the flies" (2 Kin. 1:2). And the only throne he will ever temporarily sit on will be the throne in the Third Jewish Temple, which is why the Antichrist will be instrumental in seeing it constructed during the first 3½ years of the Tribulation.

With his headquarters conveniently nestled in Jerusalem and his political position elevated to world ruler, when Satan indwells the Antichrist, he will lead him to betray Israel by breaking the peace treaty ratified with her 3½ years earlier. Scripture says, "We waited for peace, but no good came; for a time of healing, but behold, terror! From Dan is heard the snorting of his horses...the whole land quakes; for they come and devour the land and its fulness, the city and its inhabitants. 'For behold, I am sending serpents against you, adders for which there is no charm, and they will bite you,' declares the Lord" (Jer. 8:15-17).

The Antichrist will put an abrupt end to sacrifices and grain offerings. He will then enter the Third Jewish Temple, seat himself on the throne, declare himself God, and demand the world worship him (Dan. 9:27; 2 Thess. 2:4). Of this act, the Abomination of Desolation, Jesus clearly warned. He said, "When you see the Abomination of Desolation which was spoken of through Daniel the prophet, standing in the holy place, then let those who are in Judea flee to the mountains...for then there will be a great tribulation, such as has not occurred since the beginning of the world until now, nor ever shall" (Matt. 24:15, 21).

As history is destined to repeat itself, a similar event

has previously occurred in Israel's history. According to the apocryphal books of 1 and 2 Maccabees, Antiochus Epiphanes, ruler of Syria from 175 to 164 B.C., once defiled the Jewish Temple. He hated the Jews and wanted to obliterate them from the face of the earth. In 168 B.C., he invaded Israel and entered the Temple in Jerusalem. He then put a stop to the sacrificial system of worship and desecrated the Temple by placing a pig on the altar and erecting a statue of a Greek pagan God in the Holy Place. According to Jewish law, a pig is an unclean animal for sacrifice, and by offering it on the altar, it rendered the Temple abominable. Thereupon ensued the Maccabean Revolt, led by Judas Maccabees, in which thousands of Jewish men, women, and children were killed.

Likewise, Satan hates God and the Jews and all who believe in Him. He hates the Jews because through them came the Savior, the Prophets, the Scripture, the Gospel, and the Church. After he indwells the Antichrist and seats himself on the throne of God, defiling the Temple like a big pig on the altar, he will begin his worldwide persecution of the Jews and all who have accepted Christ from the beginning of the Tribulation. "When the dragon (Satan) saw that he was thrown down to the earth, he persecuted the woman (Israel) who gave birth to the male child. And the dragon was enraged with the woman, and went off to make war with the rest of her offspring, who keep the commandments of God and hold to the testimony of Jesus" (Rev. 12:13, 17, parentheses mine).

The Two Witnesses of God Killed

The first two people killed in the persecution will be the Two Witnesses of God. The Psalmist wrote, "In Thy book they were all written, the days that were ordained for me" (Ps. 139:16). Before we are even born, the number of our days are decreed, and when they are complete, God permits our deaths. Likewise, 1,260 days are allotted for the ministry of the Two Witnesses. "And when they have finished their testimony," the Antichrist himself will kill them (Rev. 11:7). He will not even afford them the dignity of a burial, but will instead order their bodies be left in the streets of Jerusalem for all the world to see. No doubt this will be viewed on television sets around the world via satellite. Because of the droughts and plagues they inflict on the earth, people will celebrate their deaths and send each other gifts. This merriment is often called the devil's Christmas. But after 3½ days, God will breathe life back into the Two Witnesses, and they will stand to their feet. Can you imagine the looks on people's faces when they see these men come to life? Scripture says, "Great fear fell upon those who were beholding them." God will then say, "Come up here," and they will ascend into a cloud before the eyes of the whole world. At that point, an earthquake will take place in Jerusalem, where a tenth of the city will fall and 7,000 people will die, and "the rest were terrified and gave glory to the God of heaven" (see Rev. 11:3-13).

The Mark of the Beast

Once the false religious figure known as the False Prophet emerges in the first half of the Tribulation, he will tirelessly point the way to the Antichrist as God. "He makes the earth and those who dwell in it to worship the beast...and he performs great signs...and he deceives those who dwell on the earth because of the signs which it was given him to perform in the presence of the beast" (Rev. 13:12-14). Along with the False Prophet, the Antichrist will also perform miraculous signs. His deception is "in accord with the activity of Satan, with all power and signs and false wonders" (2 Thess. 2:9). When he seats himself on the throne in the Temple and declares himself God, the world will initially believe him.

The False Prophet will then "tell those who dwell on the earth to make an image to the beast," and he will cause the image to speak and to kill all who do not worship the beast's image (Rev. 13:14-15). At the same time, he will administer a system whereby "the small and the great, and the rich and the poor, and the free men and the slaves (are) given a mark on their right hand, or on their forehead" (Rev. 13:16). This is referred to as the Mark of the Beast. The mark may either be the Antichrist's name or the number of his name, which totals 6-6-6. Without it, no one can buy or sell or engage in any commerce whatsoever (Rev. 13:17-18).

While the Mark of the Beast is being administered throughout the world, the third angel flying in midheaven sternly warns against receiving the mark. He cries out, saying, "If anyone worships the beast and his image, and receives a mark on his forehead or upon his hand, he will drink of the wine of the wrath of God, which is mixed in full strength in the cup of His anger; and he will be tormented with fire and brimstone in the presence of the holy angels and in the presence of the Lamb. And the smoke of their torment goes up forever and ever, and they have no rest day and night, those who worship the beast and his image, and whoever receives the mark of his name" (Rev. 14:9-11).

The mark must be received willingly; it will not be forced on anyone. But those who refuse to accept the mark will be beheaded. In the ancient Roman Empire, Christians were required to acknowledge "Caesar is Lord." The Caesars claimed to be gods. Those who refused, acknowledging "Jesus is Lord," did so at the cost of their lives. Not surprisingly, the same thing will occur under the Antichrist who emerges from a revised Roman Empire. John the apostle wrote, "...I saw the souls of those who had been beheaded because of the testimony of God, and those who had not worshiped the beast or his image, and had not received the mark upon their forehead and upon their hand" (Rev. 20:4).

Never in the history of mankind has a system of this nature been possible until now. With the use of computers and advanced scanning technology, the implementation of a bar-coded mark or biochip placed under the skin is right around the corner. The biochips contain limitless information, such as your name, date of birth, Social Security number, all the pertinent information necessary to identify an individual or transact business. It is already suggested as a method for tracking children who are lost or abducted, and governments are even considering the use of such technology on parolees.

Animal clinics currently offer microchips as a means of easily locating a lost or stolen pet. The microchips are less than an inch long and contain all the pet's medical information, as well as the name and address of its owner. Regarding this technology, Tim Willard, executive officer of the World Future Society, recently made this prophetic statement: "The technology behind such a microchip is fairly uncomplicated, and with a little refinement, it could be used in a variety of human applications. Conceivably, a number could be assigned at birth and go with a person throughout life. At the checkout stand at the supermarket, you could simply pass your hand over a scanner and your bank account would automatically be debited."[6]

Biochips implanted in humans are currently in development and will be available soon. A shocking article in the May 7, 1996, edition of the *Chicago Tribune* confirmed, "A tiny chip implanted inside the human body to send and receive radio messages...is likely to be marketed as a consumer item early in the next century. Several technologies already available or under development will enable electronics firms to make implantable ID locators, say futurists, and our yearning for convenience and security makes them almost irresistible to marketers."[7]

While biochips are not used commercially yet, we are currently utilizing Smart Cards. A Smart Card is like a credit card, except it has a chip on the inside of it. There are roughly a billion in use today, mostly in Europe and Japan, but it is growing at a rate of 30% a year, and experts forecast by the year 2001, there will be 3.4 billion in use. Their current application is in payphones, wireless phones, Internet access, banking, healthcare, and pay TV. Their benefits to consumers include the ability to efficiently manage personal finance, reduce fraud, and eliminate the need to complete time-consuming forms. Just one card can access multiple services, networks, and the Internet.

Clearly, the administration of a worldwide monetary system has never been possible until today, and the Antichrist will avail himself of this technology. Over twenty years ago, Democratic Senator Frank Church, chairman of a committee investigating activities of U.S. intelligence, stated, "The government has the technological capacity to impose 'total tyranny.' If ever a dictator came to power, there would be no place to hide."[8]

The Second 3½ Years—The Great Tribulation

> *Unless those days had been cut short, no life would have been saved....*
>
> Matthew 24:22

The prophet Jeremiah referred to this time as the "time of Jacob's trouble" (Jer. 30:7). "Jacob" refers to Israel. During this 3½-year period, two-thirds of the Jews in Israel will perish as a result of war and the Antichrist's persecution, but God has promised to bring a third of them through the fire (Zech. 13:8-9). Gentiles will also perish in the Antichrist's persecution. "A great multitude, which no one could count, from every nation and all tribes and peoples and tongues...are the ones who come out of the great tribulation" (Rev. 7:9, 14).

All who die as a result of their faith in Christ during this time will sit on thrones and reign with Him for a thousand years in His millennial kingdom. John the apostle wrote, "I saw the souls of those who had been beheaded because of the testimony of Jesus and because of the word of God, and those who had not worshiped the beast or his image, and had not received the mark upon their forehead and upon their hand; and they came to life...they will be priests of God and of Christ and will reign with Him for a thousand years" (Rev. 20:4, 6).

The Kings of the East

"The sixth angel poured out his bowl upon the great

river, the Euphrates; and its water was dried up, that the way might be prepared for the kings from the east" (Rev. 16:12). A 200-million-man army from the East will cross the Euphrates River on their way into Palestine (Rev. 9:16). The river may be dried up supernaturally or as a result of man's intervention. As stated, the Turkish government controls the Ataturk Dam, which regulates the flow of water into the Euphrates River. As Turkey is predominantly an Arab nation, they may assist the invading army in their movement into Israel. While Red China currently boasts of a 200-million-man army, the reference is to "kings," plural. Therefore, a number of Asian nations will unite to challenge the world-wide authority of the Antichrist.

The Battle of Armageddon

As previously stated, in the passage referring to the battle of Armageddon (Rev. 16:14, KJV), the Greek word used for "battle" is "polemos," meaning war or CAMPAIGN, while "mache" only signifies a battle, and in certain cases single combat. Once the War of Gog and Magog begins, the campaign will extend over the second half of the Tribulation and culminate in the battle of Armageddon.

During this second half, the nations of the world will finally wake up and realize the man they elected to rule the world is, in fact, evil incarnate, and will begin to move against his headquarters in Jerusalem in an attempt to oust him from authority.

Shortly after the midpoint, the Asian alliance will begin their movement into Palestine. Then all the nations of the world will begin to gather in the Valley of Megiddo. "The kings of the whole world...gather...together for the war of the great day of God, the Almighty...to the place which in Hebrew is called Har-Magedon" (Rev. 16:14, 16), or Armageddon. Though all the nations gather at Megiddo, the campaign of Armageddon covers the entire land of Palestine, from the plains of Esdraelon on the north (Rev. 16:16; Judg. 4, 5, 7; 1 Sam. 31:8; 2 Kin. 9:27; 23:29-30), down through Jerusalem (Zech. 12:2-11; 14:2), extending out to the valley of Jehoshaphat on the east (Joel 3:2, 13; Ezek. 39:11), and to Edom on the south (Isa. 34, 63).

The prophet Joel describes this convergence of armies into Israel. He wrote, "As the dawn is spread over the mountains, so there is a great and mighty people; there has never been anything like it, nor will there be again after it to the years of many generations" (Joel 2:2). The prophet Ezekiel likens the number of troops to "a cloud covering the land" (Ezek. 38:9, 16). In fact, blood will reach to the horses' bridles for a distance of 200 miles (Rev. 14:20), which covers most of the land of Israel from north to south.

There is little question that nuclear weapons will be used at Armageddon. A nuclear fallout will darken the skies, just as the Scriptures repeatedly warn will occur. "A day of darkness and gloom, a day of clouds and thick darkness" (Joel 2:2). "Immediately after the tribulation of those days the sun will be darkened, and the moon will not give its light, and the stars will fall from the sky, and the powers of the heavens will be shaken" (Matt. 24:29). "A day of wrath is that day, a day of trouble and distress, a day of destruction and desolation, a day of darkness and gloom, a day of clouds and thick darkness" (Zeph. 1:15). "It will come about in that day that there will be no light; the luminaries will dwindle" (Zech. 14:6).

Chemical and biological weapons of mass destruction

will also be used at Armageddon. Scripture indicates "loathsome and malignant sores" will develop on men's skin (Rev. 16:2). Anthrax causes boils and is a component of biological weapons. Nuclear warheads release radioactivity, and they will certainly cause malignant sores. Scripture gives this chilling account as well: "Now this will be the plague with which the Lord will strike all the peoples who have gone to war against Jerusalem; their flesh will rot while they stand on their feet, and their eyes will rot in their sockets, and their tongue will rot in their mouth" (Zech. 14:12).

The prophet Isaiah wrote, "Wail, for the day of the Lord...will come as destruction from the Almighty...and they will be terrified; pains and anguish will take hold of them; they will writhe like a woman in labor, they will look at one another in astonishment, their faces aflame. Behold, the day of the Lord is coming, cruel, with fury and burning anger, to make the land a desolation; and He will exterminate its sinners from it. For the stars of heaven and their constellations will not flash forth their light; the sun will be dark when it rises, and the moon will not shed its light. Thus I will punish the world for its evil, and the wicked for their iniquity...I will make mortal man scarcer than pure gold" (Isa. 13:6-12).

Finally, John the apostle described Armageddon as "flashes of lightning and sounds and peals of thunder; and there was a great earthquake, such as there had not been since man came to be upon the earth, so great an earthquake was it, and so mighty. And the great city (Jerusalem) was split into three parts, and the cities of the nations fell...and every island fled away, and the mountains were not found. And huge hailstones, about one hundred pounds each, came down from heaven upon men; and men blasphemed God because of the plague of the hail, because its plague was extremely severe"

(Rev. 16:18-21).

A third of mankind will perish by fire, smoke, and brimstone in this "war of the great day of God, the Almighty" (Rev. 9:15, 18). Though it is the final battle of the seven-year Tribulation, it is *not* the final conflict of mankind, however. That will occur when Satan is loosed at the conclusion of Christ's millennial reign.

The Second Advent of Jesus Christ

"For I will gather all the nations against Jerusalem to battle. In that day the Lord will defend the inhabitants of Jerusalem. The Lord will go forth and fight against those nations, as when He fights on a day of battle" (Zech. 14:2; 12:8; 14:3).

Just as Israel is about to be annihilated, the resplendent Lord Jesus will be seen "coming on the clouds of the sky with power and great glory" (Matt. 24:30). He and the Church will come together riding on white horses (Rev. 19:11, 14). He will also bring His holy angels with Him (Matt. 25:31; 2 Thess. 1:7-8). Israel will look up and see Jesus "whom they have pierced; and they will mourn for Him, as one mourns for an only son, and they will weep bitterly over Him, like the bitter weeping over a first-born" (Zech. 12:10). Imagine their shock, amazement, and heartbreak when Israel realizes for the first time that they crucified their own Savior.

When the Lord returns, "His feet will stand on the Mount of Olives, which is in front of Jerusalem on the east; and the Mount of Olives will be split in its middle from east to west by a very large valley, so that half of the mountain will move toward the north and the other half toward the south"

(Zech. 14:4). This relates to the great earthquake at Armageddon where "the great city (Jerusalem) was split into three parts" (Rev. 16:19). The glorious Lord Jesus is described as having eyes as a flame of fire, wearing many crowns, and a name is written on Him which no one knows but Himself (Rev. 19:12), and written across the thigh of His robe will be the words "KING OF KINGS, AND LORD OF LORDS" (Rev. 19:16).

Incredibly, when the Lord appears, the Antichrist and all the armies of the nations gathered in Israel will turn to fight against Jesus and the saints and angels. "And I saw the beast and the kings of the earth and their armies, assembled to make war against Him...and against His army" (Rev. 19:19).

It goes without saying our magnificent Lord and Savior "will overcome them, because He is Lord of lords and King of kings" (Rev. 17:14). The Antichrist and False Prophet will be seized and thrown alive into the eternal lake of fire. "The beast was seized, and with him the false prophet...these two were thrown alive into the lake of fire...and the rest were killed with the sword which came from the mouth of Him who sat upon the horse" (Rev. 19:20-21). By the word of His mouth He creates, and by the word of His mouth He destroys.

And as for Satan, he gets to twiddle his thumbs in the abyss for a thousand years. "And I saw an angel coming down from heaven, having the key of the abyss and a great chain in his hand. And he laid hold of the dragon, the serpent of old, who is the devil and Satan, and bound him for a thousand years, and threw him into the abyss, and shut it and sealed it over him, so that he should not deceive the nations any longer, until the thousand years were completed" (Rev. 20:1-3). As ruler of the demonic world, when Satan is bound, the demons will be subdued as well.

Satan will be taunted while he sits in the abyss. "'Sheol from beneath is excited over you to meet you when you come; it arouses for you the spirits of the dead, all the leaders of the earth; it raises all the kings of the nations from their thrones. They will all respond and say to you, 'Even you have been made weak as we, you have become like us. Your pomp and the music of your harps have been brought down to Sheol; maggots are spread out as your bed beneath you, and worms are your covering'" (Isa. 14:9-11).

> *The God of peace will soon crush Satan under your feet.*
>
> Romans 16:20

The Second Advent Resurrection and Judgment Program

As previously stated, the Tribulation is divided into two halves, each lasting exactly 1,260 days. But Daniel wrote that from when the Abomination of Desolation is set up, which is at the midpoint, there will be 1,290 days, and then he adds, "How blessed is he who keeps waiting and attains to the 1,335 days" (Dan. 12:11-12). The additional time amounts to 75 days, and it is placed after the battle of Armageddon but before the Millennium begins. Jesus said, "Behold, I am coming quickly, and My reward is with Me, to render to every man according to what he has done" (Rev. 22:12). It is during this 75-day period after the Second Advent that the resurrection and judgment program will take place.

It is hard to imagine how anyone will survive the Tribulation, but there will be a scant few from among Israel and the nations who will enter the Millennium in their physical state to receive the promises of God and to repopulate the earth. But before Christ's righteous millennial reign can begin, it must be determined whether these people are saved because *no unsaved person* will enter the Millennium. Scripture is clear: "Truly, truly, I say to you, unless one is born again, he cannot see the kingdom of God" (John 3:3). And again, "Unless you are converted...you shall not enter the kingdom of heaven" (Matt. 18:3). So at the end of the Tribulation, there will be the Judgment of Israel and the Judgment of Gentile Nations to determine salvation of those who survived. But first, there will be the resurrection of all the righteous from the beginning of Creation.

The Resurrection Program

The physical body of every person who has ever lived and died will someday be resurrected and reunited with their spirit. Some will come out of the grave to the resurrection of life, while others will come out of the grave to the resurrection of damnation. Once we reach the age of accountability, an age which only God knows, we are responsible for making the choice which determines the resurrection of which we will be a part.

Except for those who survive the Tribulation, every saint from Adam onward will enter the Millennium in their bodies, tranformed into a glorified state, the same state Jesus was after He rose from the grave. He could be touched and felt, but could also walk through walls (John 20:19-29). He was in His glorified state. The apostle Paul wrote, "The dead will be raised imperishable, and we shall be changed. For this perishable must put on the imperishable, and this mortal must put on immortality" (1 Cor. 15:52-53).

Our present bodies are quite different from those we shall inhabit in our glorified state. Paul wrote, "There are heavenly bodies and earthly bodies, but the glory of the heavenly is one, and the glory of the earthly is another. There is one glory of the sun, and another glory of the moon, and another glory of the stars; for star differs from star in glory. So also is the resurrection of the dead. It is sown a perishable body, it is raised an imperishable body; it is sown in dishonor, it is raised in glory; it is sown in weakness, it is raised in power; it is sown a natural body, it is raised a spiritual body. If there is a natural body, there is also a spiritual body" (1 Cor. 15:40-44). He adds, "Just as we have borne the image of the earthy, we shall also bear the image of the heavenly" (1 Cor. 15:49).

The Lord Jesus was the first to be resurrected and transformed and will be followed by the Church-age saints at the Rapture. At that time, the bodies of all believers who died from Pentecost forward to the Rapture will be resurrected and reunited with their spirits in the air. Scripture says, "For if we believe that Jesus died and rose again, even so God will *bring with Him* those who have fallen asleep in Jesus. And the dead in Christ shall rise first" (1 Thess. 4:14, 16, italics mine). This means their bodies will rise out of the grave to meet their spirits in the air. All believers who are alive and fortunate enough to experience the Rapture will not face physical death, but will rather be instantly changed into this glorified state. "Behold, I tell you a mystery; we shall not all sleep, but we shall all be changed, in a moment, in the twinkling of an eye" (1 Cor. 15:51-52).

Just as "each one of us shall give account of himself to God" (Rom. 14:12), the Church-age saints will be the first group to face judgment at the Judgment Seat of Christ while the Tribulation is taking place on earth. There, believers will be judged for faithful service while on earth and rewarded accordingly (Rom. 14:10; 1 Cor. 3:11-15; 2 Cor. 5:10).

So after Jesus returns to earth at the Second Advent, but before "the saints go marching in" to His millennial kingdom, yet two more groups of believers will to be resurrected and judged. Scripture says, "The time came for the dead to be judged, and the time to give their reward to Thy bond-servants the prophets and to the saints and to those who fear Thy name, the small and the great" (Rev. 11:18).

Remember, *everyone* will bow before Christ, and *everyone* will confess Jesus as Lord to the glory of God (Phil. 2:10-11).

The Old Testament Saints

When the Rapture happens, the Old Testament saints will not be included with the Church-age saints. Scripture says, "The Lord Himself will descend from heaven with a shout...and the dead *in Christ* shall rise first. Then we who are alive and remain shall be caught up together with them in the clouds to meet the Lord in the air" (1 Thess. 4:16-17, italics mine). Of course, the Old Testament saints preceded Christ's incarnation, so they are not Raptured with the Church.

They are, in fact, resurrected and judged at the end of the Tribulation after Jesus returns to earth. The prophet Daniel was told that after the "time of distress such as never occurred since there was a nation until that time," many of his people "who sleep in the dust of the ground will awake." He is then told to "go your way to the end; then you will enter into rest and rise again for your allotted portion at the end of the age"

(Dan. 12:1, 2, 13).

The prophet Ezekiel was given a vision of a valley full of very dry bones. God tells the bones, "Behold, I will cause breath to enter you that you may come to life. And I will put sinews on you, make flesh grow back on you, cover you with skin, and put breath in you that you may come alive" (Ezek. 37:5-6). He then tells Ezekiel the meaning of the vision. "These bones are the whole house of Israel...behold, I will open your graves and cause you to come up out of your graves, My people; and I will bring you into the land of Israel...and I will put My Spirit within you, and you will come to life...." (Ezek. 37:11-12, 14)

Only believing Israel will be resurrected at that time to enter the Millennium. There will be many who will awake to "disgrace and everlasting contempt" (Dan. 12:2) at the Great White Throne Judgment.

The Tribulation Saints

Finally, the bodies of the "great multitude, which no one could count, from every nation and all tribes and peoples and tongues...who come out of the great tribulation (Rev. 7:9, 14), must also be resurrected and judged before their entry into the Millennium. This takes place at the Second Advent as well. "And I saw the souls of those who had been beheaded because of the testimony of Jesus and because of the word of God...and they came to life and reigned with Christ for a thousand years" (Rev. 20:4).

So the program at Christ's Second Advent provides for all the remaining righteous from the beginning of creation to be resurrected, judged, and transformed into their glorified states before entry into the Millennium. After this, one final resurrection of the dead will take place. The only group remaining are the unsaved dead, or the wicked dead from the beginning of Creation. Their bodies will continue to stay in the grave until after the Millennium, when they will be resurrected to stand before God at the Great White Throne Judgment (Rev. 20:11-15).

At the conclusion of the Tribulation, every saint will have faced judgment except for those who survive the Tribulation, and now they must face judgment and their salvation be determined before entry into the Millennium because, again, no one enters unsaved. These are the ones who will repopulate the earth.

The Judgment Program

Scripture says, "When the Son of Man comes in His glory, and all the angels with Him, then He will sit on His glorious throne. And all the nations will be gathered before Him" (Matt. 25:31). It further states, "His winnowing fork is in His hand, and He will thoroughly clear His threshing floor; and He will gather His wheat into the barn, but He will burn up the chaff with unquenchable fire" (Matt. 3:12).

Judgment of Israel

As the nations go, Israel will be first in the order of judgment. At the Second Advent when Jesus returns to earth, He will gather all the Jews scattered from around the world and bring them supernaturally into Israel. Scripture says, "He will send forth His angels with a great trumpet and they will gather together His elect from the four winds, from one end of the sky to the other" (Matt. 24:31). The Lord will bring the

Jews into Israel to determine who are saved and who are not.

Once this has been determined, those who believed on the Lord Jesus will enter the Millennium; those who did not will be killed. The prophet Ezekiel wrote, "'I shall bring you out from the peoples and gather you from the lands where you are scattered, with a mighty hand and with an outstretched arm and with wrath poured out; and I shall bring you into the wilderness of the peoples, and there I shall enter into judgment with you face to face. As I entered into judgment with your fathers in the wilderness of the land of Egypt, so I will enter into judgment with you,' declares the Lord God. 'And I shall make you pass under the rod, and I shall bring you into the bond of the covenant; and I shall purge from you the rebels and those who transgress against Me; I shall bring them out of the land where they sojourn, but they will not enter the land of Israel'" (Ezek. 20:34-38).

Israel's judgment is depicted in the parable of the ten virgins (Matt. 25:1-13). In this parable, there are five virgins who are prepared and awaiting the arrival of their bridegroom and five who are not. When the announcement is made that the bridegroom is approaching, the five who are unprepared miss his appearance, while the five prepared virgins go into the wedding feast with him. The wedding feast is symbolic of the Millennium.

Israel's judgment is again depicted in the parable of the talents (Matt. 25:14-30). This parable concerns the rewards which are meted out to those who are faithful. In this parable, a man about to go on a journey entrusts his possessions to three of his servants, expecting them to multiply that which he gives them, each according to his own ability. One is given five talents, or units of money, one is given two talents, and one is given one talent. When the man returns from his journey, two of the servants are rewarded for doubling their master's money, while the servant who received one talent does nothing and hides it in the ground. He is symbolic of a man who had the possibility of salvation but chose wickedness instead. He is therefore cast into the outer darkness where there is weeping and gnashing of teeth.

This time of Israel's judgment is what the apostle Paul referred to when he said "all Israel will be saved" (Rom. 11:26). He adds, "The Deliverer will come from Zion, He will remove ungodliness from Jacob" (Rom. 11:26). The Jews will be brought into Israel to pass under the rod of judgment. Those who rebel and transgress against the Lord will be purged from those who believe, and thereby, all of Israel who enter the Millennium will indeed be saved.

Judgment of Gentile Nations

The 20th century has already witnessed the offals of evil incarnate. During World War II, Adolf Hitler and his Third Reich slaughtered six million Jews and countless others who did not fit his Arian agenda. But there were brave German citizens who risked their own lives to help those fleeing Hitler's persecution. The Antichrist's massacre of the Jews will be worldwide, and like so many German citizens, there will be those in all the nations who will attempt to shelter and protect the fleeing Jews. Though this judgment will encompass the nations, salvation will be determined on an individual basis. Again, their works do not save them, but rather, distinguish the saved from the unsaved.

The Judgment of Gentile Nations is depicted in the sheep and goat judgment (Matt. 25:31-46). In this passage, the sheep represent the saved, while the goats represent the unsaved. The Lord places the sheep on His right and the goats on His left. He tells the sheep to enter His millennial kingdom because they fed Him, gave Him something to drink, invited Him in as a stranger, clothed Him, visited Him when He was sick and when He was in prison. But they do not understand and question when they did all of this for Him. The Lord responds by saying, "Truly I say to you, to the extent that you did it to one of these brothers of Mine, even to the least of them, you did it to Me" (Matt. 25:40). He then commands the goats on His left to depart from Him into eternal punishment because when His brothers came to them in the same manner, the goats did nothing to help.

Scripture says, "It is only just for God to repay with affliction those who afflict you, and to give relief to you who are afflicted...when the Lord Jesus shall be revealed from heaven with His mighty angels in flaming fire, dealing out retribution to those who do not know God and to those who do not obey the gospel of our Lord Jesus. These will pay the penalty of eternal destruction away from the presence of the Lord and from the glory of His power, when He comes to be glorified in His saints on that day, and to be marveled at among all who have believed" (2 Thess. 1:6-10).

Once the Tribulation is finally over, sin and rebellion will be purged from the earth. All the righteous will have been resurrected and judged, the survivors will have faced their judgment, and the Lord Jesus will begin His righteous reign on earth for a thousand years.

Now to the King eternal, immortal, invisible, the only God, be honor and glory forever and ever. Amen.

1 Timothy 1:17

Endnotes

1) As quoted by William R. Goetz, *Apocalypse Next,* (Horizon Books, Camp Hill, Pennsylvania, 1996) pp. 214-215.
2) J. Dwight Pentecost, *Things to Come,* (Zondervan Publishing House, Grand Rapids, Michigan, 1958) p. 340.
3) Ibid., pp. 326-327.
4) Ibid., p. 330.
5) As quoted by William R. Goetz, *Apocalypse Next,* (Horizon Books, Camp Hill, Pennsylvania, 1996) p. 214.
6) Jack Van Impe, *2001: On The Edge of Eternity,* (Word Publishing, Dallas, Texas, 1996) p. 76.
7) Ibid., p. 124.
8) As quoted by William R. Goetz, *Apocalypse Next,* (Horizon Books, Camp Hill, Pennsylvania, 1996) p. 206.

To Him was given dominion, glory and a kingdom, that all the peoples, nations, and men of every language might serve Him. His dominion is an everlasting dominion which will not pass away; and His kingdom is one which will not be destroyed.

Daniel 7:14

Chapter 8

The MILLENNIUM

Though we are fast approaching the end of the second MILLENNIUM, all references in this writing to the MILLENNIUM have been to Christ's 1,000-year reign on earth. Even if the Church were Raptured today, the seven-year Tribulation must follow before the return of Christ to earth, and therefore, THE APPROACHING TURN OF THE MILLENNIUM SHOULD NOT BE CONFUSED WITH THE COMMENCEMENT OF CHRIST'S MILLENNIAL REIGN. Indeed, Jesus will return in the next MILLENNIUM, but the two millennial references have no connection and are not used interchangeably.

As previously stated, the MILLENNIUM will be primarily instituted for the fulfillment of God's covenants made with the nation of Israel. They are the Abrahamic covenant, the Palestinic covenant, and the Davidic covenant. The MILLENNIUM will also be established to demonstrate the fallen nature of humanity. With Satan bound in the abyss for a thousand years and the demonic world subdued with him, the source of external temptation will be removed. Yet the wickedness within man's heart will prevail, as we shall see, at the conclusion of the MILLENNIUM.

A Theocratic Kingdom

A theocracy is a government established under divine guidance. The governing Authority during the MILLENNIUM will be the glorious Lord Jesus Himself (Ps. 2:6-9; Ps. 72; Isa. 9:6-7). He will reign over the whole earth (Ps. 47:8; Isa. 24:23; Zech. 14:9), and David will rule with Him over the nation of Israel (Jer. 30:9; 33:15-17; Ezek. 34:23-24; 37:24-25; Hos. 3:5).

Under David, there will also be rulers, including the twelve disciples who will "sit upon twelve thrones, judging the twelve tribes of Israel" (Isa. 32:1; Jer. 30:21; Matt. 19:28). It is important to note Judas is not one of these twelve disciples. In fact, Jesus said of Judas, "Woe to that man by whom the Son of Man is betrayed! It would have been good for that man if he had not been born" (Matt. 26:24). After Judas hung himself for his betrayal of Jesus, the disciples cast lots for who was to fill the vacancy, and it fell to Matthias, who was then counted with the eleven (see Acts 1:16-26).

There will be other subordinate levels of authority as well, all of whom answer to the Lord. Jesus used a parable to describe those who are faithful ruling over cities as a reward for their faithfulness (see Luke 19:11-27). And all who are martyred during the Tribulation will also reign with Him on thrones (Rev. 20:4, 6).

In this kingdom, the government will not tolerate sin. With the indwelling Spirit, the knowledge and presence of the Lord, and the removal of external temptation, there is no excuse for sin, and it will therefore be punishable by death (Ps. 2:9; Isa. 29:20-21). "Everyone will die for his own iniquity" (Jer. 31:30).

"The Lord reigns...He will judge the peoples with equity" (Ps. 96:10). The Lord's rule will be righteous and just (Isa. 2:3-4; 11:2-5; 32:1). In His kingdom, Jesus is seen as King and Priest. Therefore, Church and State will be one (Ps. 110:1-7; Isa. 66:23; Ezek. 37:26-28; Zech. 14:16-19).

Israel in the Kingdom

At the end of the Tribulation, all of the surviving Jews scattered throughout the world will be supernaturally gathered and brought into Israel (Isa. 27:12; 43:5-7; Jer. 12:15; 24:6; Ezek. 28:25-26; Mic. 4:6; Zeph. 3:20; Matt. 24:31). At that time, their salvation will be determined before entry into the MILLENNIUM. The Jews will be restored to their land where they will receive the blessings of the covenants God promised their forefathers.

God promised Abraham that in him, all the families of the earth would be blessed, that his descendants would be given Canaan as an everlasting possession, that his descendants would multiply like the dust of the earth, and that they would all worship God (Gen. 12:1-3; 12:6-7; 13:14-17; 15:1-21; 17:1-14; 22:15-18).

Through the Palestinic covenant, God promised that Israel would fully repent, that all would be converted, and that the Lord would return and restore them to their land (Deut. 30:1-10). It appears Israel's conversion will be a sovereign act of God in keeping with His promise. This covenant served as an extension to the Abrahamic covenant in that it also provided the basis upon which the land of Canaan would someday be occupied by Abraham's descendants.

Finally, God promised David that a child (Solomon) would be born to him who would establish his kingdom and build the temple, and that David's house, throne, and kingdom would last forever (2 Sam. 7:12-16).

During the MILLENNIUM, all these covenants with Israel will be fulfilled. The nation was joined to God by marriage (Ezek. 16:8-14), and at this time, their relationship to Him as their Husband will be renewed (Isa. 54:5-7; 62:2-5; Hos. 2:19-20). As the chosen of God, Israel will also be exalted over the Gentiles (Isa. 14:1-2; 49:22-23). "The sons of those who afflicted you will come bowing to you, and all those who despised you will bow themselves at the soles of your feet; and they will call you the city of the Lord, the Zion of the Holy One of Israel" (Isa. 60:14).

Because of the ruin of Palestine during the latter half of the Tribulation, Israel will be reconstructed during this time (Isa. 61:4; Ezek. 36:33-38; Amos 9:14), and its borders extended to include all the land promised to Abraham (Gen. 15:18-21; Isa. 26:15; Obad. 19-20). The twelve tribes of Israel will each receive their apportioned land, including the tribe of Dan (Ezek. 48:1-29). And the "holy oblation," a squared territory consisting of 34 miles in each direction, will be set apart for the Lord (Ezek. 48:8-20).

Gentiles in the Kingdom

All the surviving Gentiles at the conclusion of the Tribulation will face judgment to determine their salvation before entry into the MILLENNIUM. Those who are saved will enter and inherit the universal blessings of the Abrahamic covenant. The apostle Paul wrote, "If you belong to Christ, then you are Abraham's offspring, heirs according to promise" (Gal. 3:29). All will be under the Lordship of Jesus as King, and for a thousand years, the Gentiles will be second to the Jews, who are given favor by God during this period (Isa. 14:1-2; 49:22-23; 60:14).

Spiritual Life in the Kingdom

The born-again who survived the Tribulation will enter the MILLENNIUM in their physical bodies to repopulate the earth (Isa. 26:2; 60:21; Matt. 25:37). Of course, children who have not reached the age of accountability will also enter, but personal faith in Christ will be required of them and their descendants, who will be born with a sin nature (Jer. 30:29). Once they receive Christ, the Holy Spirit will indwell them as believers. There are a number of Scripture references which relate to the indwelling Spirit during the MILLENNIUM (Isa. 32:15; 44:3; 59:21; Ezek. 36:26-27; 37:14; 39:29; Joel 2:28-29).During this period, spiritual life will be different than at any other time since Creation. There will be universal spiritual truth, the knowledge of God throughout the world (Jer. 31:34). Jesus will dwell among man (Ezek. 37:28-29; Zech. 2:10-13; Rev. 21:3), and the whole earth will be filled with the glory of God (Ps. 72:19). Satan will be bound and the demonic world will be restrained, so there will be nothing evil to influence man's heart. The earth will be full of righteousness. "The Lord God will cause righteousness and praise to spring up before all the nations" (Isa. 61:11). It will be a time of willing obedience to the Lord, a time of joy inexpressible, a time of heartfelt passion for the Lord.

Unlike the numerous religions which exist today, there will be one faith. All the world will be united in worshiping the Lord God (Isa. 45:23; 52:10; 66:20-23; Zeph. 3:9; Zech. 14:16; Mal. 1:11).

The Millennial Temple

Ezekiel went into great detail in describing the millennial Temple. He also described the throne, the altar, priestly service, and worship rituals (Ezek. 40:1-46:24). The Lord Jesus will reign over the world from this Temple (Ezek. 43:7), built on the 34-square-mile site of the "holy oblation." It will be 875 feet in length and width, towering three stories high, with thirty rooms on each level (Ezek. 41:5-7). It will face in an easterly direction and be completely surrounded by a wall, with gates on all sides but the west. Just on the inside of the wall will be the outer courtyard, where the people will assemble. There will also be an elevated inner courtyard, accessible by three gates, all of which are opposite the gates in the outer wall. The Lord declared, "This is the place of My throne and the place of the soles of My feet, where I will dwell among the sons of Israel forever" (Ezek. 43:7).

During the MILLENNIUM, worship rituals will resume to include animal sacrifices through burnt offerings, sin offerings, and guilt offerings (Isa. 56:7; Jer. 33:18; Ezek. 40:39; 46:13). This sacrificial system will not be established for the atonement of sin, but as a memorial to the accomplished work of redemption.

Everyday Life in the Kingdom

It appears the organizational structure and routine of life will continue in the MILLENNIUM much as it does today, except man will live in a near-perfect environment under a righteous King and Priest. As such, the established order of things will be fully under His control, and sin will not be tolerated. For a thousand years, our Lord will showcase to the world and to the universe what life could have been like all this time in the beautiful state which God intended. There are a number of Scripture references which characterize what everyday life will be like in the millennial kingdom. Here are just a few.

There will finally be lasting peace on earth. "The work of righteousness will be peace, and the service of righteousness, quietness and confidence forever" (Isa. 32:17).

There will be night and day, but the light of both will be brilliant. "The light of the moon will be as the light of the sun, and the light of the sun will be seven times brighter, like the light of seven days" (Isa. 30:26).

There will be no more sickness. "No resident will say, 'I am sick'" (Isa. 33:24). "'I will restore you to health and I will heal you of your wounds,' declares the Lord" (Jer. 30:17). Before entry into the MILLENNIUM, He will correct any deformities. "On that day the deaf shall hear words of a book, and out of their gloom and darkness the eyes of the blind shall see" (Isa. 29:17).

Society will be industrialized. "They shall build houses and inhabit them; they shall also plant vineyards and eat their fruit" (Isa. 65:21).

There will be economic prosperity for everyone. "They shall come and shout for joy on the height of Zion, and they shall be radiant over the bounty of the Lord, over the grain, and the new wine, and the oil, and over the young of the flock and the herd; and their life shall be like a watered garden, and they shall never languish again...I will turn their mourning into joy, and will comfort them, and give them joy for their sorrow" (Jer. 31:12-13).

Just as before the Flood, *lifespans will be lengthened.* "No longer will there be in it an infant who lives but a few days, or an old man who does not live out his days; for the youth will die at the age of one hundred and the one who does not reach the age of one hundred shall be thought accursed" (Isa. 65:20).

Lastly, *the animal kingdom will be changed.* "The wolf will dwell with the lamb, and the leopard will lie down with the kid, and the calf and the young lion and the fatling together; and a little boy will lead them. Also the cow and the bear will graze; their young will lie down together; and the lion will eat straw like the ox. And the nursing child will play by the hole of the cobra, and the weaned child will put his hand on the viper's den. They will not hurt or destroy in all My holy mountain, for the earth will be full of the knowledge of the Lord as the waters cover the sea" (Isa. 11:6-9).

The Heavenly Jerusalem

Scripture says, "You have come to Mount Zion and to the city of the living God, the heavenly Jerusalem, and to myriads of angels, to the general assembly and church of the first-born who are enrolled in heaven, and to God, the Judge of all, and to the spirits of righteous men made perfect, and to Jesus, the mediator of a new covenant" (Heb. 12:22-23).

We have seen at the conclusion of the Tribulation that there will be a program of resurrection and judgment. At that time the bodies of all the righteous before the Day of Pentecost as well as those of the Tribulation martyrs will be resurrected and reunited with their spirits to face judgment and receive their eternal rewards. We saw that the Church-age saints will have experienced this seven years earlier at the Rapture, where they will then stand in heaven before the Judgment Seat of Christ to receive their eternal rewards.

All of these saints will have been translated into their glorified bodies, and together with the holy angels, this mighty assembly will enter the MILLENNIUM where they will live in the heavenly Jerusalem. It appears that at the Second Advent when the Lord Jesus returns to earth, the heavenly Jerusalem will descend (Rev. 21:10) and hover over the earth where Jerusalem is today.

The living saints who will have survived the Tribulation will enter the MILLENNIUM in their natural bodies, where they will continue to live on the earth and repopulate it. They will not be able to enter the heavenly Jerusalem, for only those living in glorified states can enter. But this is not so for the translated saints, who can freely come and go from the heavenly Jerusalem to earth. Just as Jesus walked among men in His glorified state after His resurrection, so will the translated saints walk among the living saints on the earth during the MILLENNIUM.

As part of the governing body in the Lord's theocratic kingdom, the translated saints will sit on thrones in various capacities and judge the world. The apostle Paul wrote, "Do you not know that the saints will judge the world?" (1 Cor. 6:2). During the MILLENNIUM, only those living on the earth will be subject to the Lord's reign, not those living in the heavenly Jerusalem. These translated saints will have already been brought under His authority, and as such, will be part of His administration of righteousness.

As Jesus approached Jerusalem nearly 2,000 years ago, He gave the parable of a nobleman who was going away to a distant country to receive a kingdom (Luke 19:11-27). Once he received it, he would return. So he called his servants and gave them each a sum of money to conduct business while he was away. When he returned, he summoned them to see what business they had done. One earned ten times the amount he was given, to which the nobleman replied, "Well done," adding, "because you have been faithful in a very little thing, be in authority over ten cities." Each who increased his money was granted authority over cities equal in number to what he had earned. This parable was used to show the rewards for servitude, and likewise applies to the faithful saints, who will be given authority over many cities when the King returns.

At the end of the MILLENNIUM, it appears the heavenly Jerusalem and all its occupants will ascend back into heaven as God destroys the earth for the final time.

> *Thy Kingdom come; Thy will be done, on earth as it is in heaven.*
>
> Matthew 6:10

Chapter 9

After the MILLENNIUM, Then What?

The Second War of Gog and Magog

Though man will live in a near-perfect environment for a thousand years, in the presence of the Lord Jesus and with the full knowledge of God, there will be a final uprising which will attest to the sinful, wicked nature of the human heart, a heart which can only be changed by the grace of God when we receive a new nature through salvation. This war is the final conflict for mankind. It will occur at the conclusion of the thousand-year reign of Christ, and the participants will be "like the sand of the seashore" (Rev. 20:8).

Before the MILLENNIUM begins, Satan will be bound in chains and thrown into the abyss where he will stay for a thousand years (Rev. 20:1-3). But "when the thousand years are completed, Satan will be released from his prison, and will come out to deceive the nations which are in the four corners of the earth, Gog and Magog, to gather them together for the war" (Rev. 20:7-8).

This war is not to be confused with the one occurring

around the midpoint of the Tribulation, as recorded in Ezekiel 38 and 39. There is uncertainty as to why two wars of the same name occur, but clearly a number of differences exist between the two. Ezekiel describes a coalition of only a few nations invading Israel; whereas in the second war, all the nations are gathered against Jerusalem. Ezekiel records Gog's alliance on the northern mountains of Israel; whereas in this second war, the participants are on the broad plain surrounding Jerusalem. Ezekiel makes no mention of Satan's direct intervention; whereas in the second war, he is the catalyst for the uprising. Ezekiel records Gog's destruction by forces of nature, combined with man-made weapons of destruction, and afterward, a period of seven months to bury the dead and seven years to dispose of the debris. In this second war, the invaders are consumed by fire "which came down from heaven and devoured them" (Rev. 20:9), leaving no bodies to be buried. Ezekiel records the millennial kingdom to follow; whereas after the second war, no life continues, but rather, the heavens and the earth are totally destroyed.

Scripture does not indicate how long the war will last, only that after Satan has been bound for a thousand years, "he must be released for a short time" (Rev. 20:3).

Judgment on Satan and the Fallen Angels

After Satan's release and final attempt to overthrow God, he will be cast into the eternal lake of fire (Rev. 20:10), as his earthly kingdom finally comes to an end. He will then no longer be the prince and power of the air. The Antichrist and False Prophet will have already been in the lake of fire a thousand years when Satan joins them. There, they will be "tormented day and night forever and ever" (Rev. 19:20; 20:10).

But judgment still awaits the angels who followed Satan in his rebellion against God. Scripture says, "Angels who did not keep their own domain, but abandoned their proper abode, He has kept in eternal bonds under darkness for the judgment of the great day" (Jude 6). The apostle Peter wrote, "God did not spare angels when they sinned, but cast them into hell and committed them to pits of darkness, reserved for judgment" (2 Pet. 2:4). When Satan is cast into the lake of fire, his minions will be thrown in there with him. Their judgment is one I surely hope to see.

The New Heavens and the New Earth

The Satanically led revolt against God at the conclusion of the MILLENNIUM will bring the armies of the world again to Jerusalem where God will consume them by fire. At that point, He will also destroy the world by fire. The apostle Peter wrote, "The present heavens and earth by His word are being reserved for fire, kept for the day of judgment and destruction of ungodly men. The heavens will pass away with a roar and the elements will be destroyed with intense heat, and the earth and its works will be burned up" (2 Pet. 3:7, 10).

Because Adam and Eve sinned in the Garden of Eden, a curse was placed on the earth by God (Gen. 3:17; 5:29). Scripture says, "The creation was subjected to futility, not of its own will, but because of Him who subjected it, in hope that the creation itself also will be set free from its slavery to corruption into the freedom of the glory of the children of God. For we know that the whole creation groans and suffers the pains of childbirth together until now" (Rom. 8:20-22).

Simply put, sin defiles everything, and by God's very nature, He cannot be in the presence of sin. So before God Himself makes His dwelling among men (Rev. 21:3), the earth must be destroyed and reformed in purity. Our infinite God will create another earth for Himself and His family.

John the apostle wrote, "I saw a new heaven and a new earth; for the first heaven and the first earth passed away" (Rev. 21:1). And God said, "Behold, I am making all things new" (Rev. 21:5).

The Great White Throne Judgment

Once the earth is purged, the unsaved dead will stand before God at the Great White Throne Judgment. "And I saw a great white throne and Him who sat upon it, from whose presence earth and heaven fled away, and no place was found for them" (Rev. 20:11). This is the final resurrection and judgment. Remember, before entry into Christ's millennial kingdom, every righteous person from the beginning of Creation will face their day of judgment. At that point, the only ones who remain to be judged are the unsaved dead, those who did not choose life through Jesus Christ or put their faith in God before Pentecost.

How many of us have heard someone say, "If I'm going to hell, at least my friends will be there"? It grieves me to know there will be good people there who did not see the importance of choosing Jesus Christ while they were alive. They did not understand or accept the reality of the atonement of sin through His blood, and they died forever separated from Him. Hell is a place of consciousness, and they will remember all the times someone told them of Jesus and what He did for them on the Cross. The only reason God entered this world in the form of a man was "to seek and to save that which was lost" (Luke 19:10). That was you, that was me, that was all of us before we responded to His love. He calls everyone, but He has given us a free will to decide for ourselves whether we will respond and invite Him into our hearts. He says, "Behold, I stand at the door and knock; if anyone hears My voice and opens the door, I will come in to him, and will dine with him, and he with Me" (Rev. 3:20).

So many people get hung up on "I can't believe a loving God will send all these billions of people to hell because they don't believe as Christians do." The fact of the matter is, He is not sending anyone to hell. We send ourselves to hell. *Everyone* has the opportunity to come to Him, *everyone*. Scripture says, "God is not one to show partiality, but in every nation the man who fears Him and does what is right, is welcome to Him" (Acts 10:34-35). And "*whoever* will call upon the name of the Lord will be saved" (Rom. 10:13, italics mine).

We cannot live any way we want. There are eternal consequences to our actions, and if you choose to live your short life on this earth "and not respond to His lovc," then do not be fooled into believing when you die, you will spend eternity with a holy God. Contrary to what the world tells you, life is not about the pursuit of happiness, but the pursuit of pleasing God. We were created for His good pleasure (Rev. 4:11), and we should "have as our ambition...to be pleasing to Him" (2 Cor. 5:9). A rightstanding relationship with the Lord then creates a heart overflowing with joy, even in the midst of difficult circumstances.

Indeed, there will be more people in hell than in heaven. Jesus said, "Enter by the narrow gate; for the gate is wide, and the way is broad that leads to destruction, and many are those who enter by it. For the gate is small, and the way is narrow that leads to life, and few are those who find it" (Matt. 7:13-14).

When the unsaved die, their bodies go to the grave, while their spirits descend into hell, a place of torment. However, Hell is not the final resting place for the wicked dead. At the Great White Throne Judgment, the bodies of the unsaved are resurrected and reunited with their spirits to stand before God. For a brief moment in time, they will have a reprieve from their torment to stand in His all-consuming, holy presence where they too will bow their knees and confess Jesus as Lord (Phil. 2:10-11). Once they are judged, they will be cast into the lake of fire, where they will stay forever. Scripture says, "And I saw a great white throne and Him who sat upon it...and I saw the dead, the great and the small, standing before the throne, and the books were opened, and another book was opened, which is the book of life; and the dead were judged from the things which were written in the books, according to their deeds...and if anyone's name was not found written in the book of life, he was thrown into the lake of fire" (Rev. 20:11-12, 15).

When we choose Jesus Christ as our personal Savior, He comes to take up residence in our hearts through the Holy Spirit (John 14:16-17; Rom. 8:11; Eph. 3:16-17). At that very moment, our names are recorded in the Book of Life forever. As human beings, we are so limited by time that we cannot conceive of time never ending, but be assured, each one of us will live eternally either with God or separated from Him, and when a billion years has passed, then there will be another billion, and then another, and another.

Dear reader, *please listen.* Someday, *you are going to*

die, but you do not know when your soul will be required of you. So "today, if you would hear His voice, do not harden your hearts" (Ps. 95:7-8). If you have not already done so, then right now, get on your knees and acknowledge Jesus as Lord, that you realize He came to pay the price for sin, and that you are a sinner in need of forgiveness. Ask Him to forgive you of your sins and invite Him to come into your heart.

If you are sincere, He will take up residence within you through the Holy Spirit (John 14:16-17; 2 Tim. 1:14), and you will slowly begin to change into conformity to His likeness. Scripture says, "If you confess with your mouth Jesus as Lord, and believe in your heart that God raised Him from the dead, you shall be saved; for with the heart man believes, resulting in righteousness, and with the mouth he confesses, resulting in salvation" (Rom. 10:9-10). You will experience life abundantly, and most assuredly, you will be spared the Great White Throne Judgment.

The New Jerusalem

With a newly created heaven and earth, the eternal city of the New Jerusalem will descend to earth. It is not possible to describe our eternal abode and do it justice, but one thing is sure, "Things which eye has not seen and ear has not heard, and which have not entered the heart of man, all that God has prepared for those who love Him" (1 Cor. 2:9).

Close your eyes for a moment and picture the most pristine thing you have ever seen. Perhaps it is a place high in the mountains, a place you have found where not a hint of civilization has been. Or maybe it was a sunset so brilliant you stopped what you were doing to gaze at what looked like fire in the sky. Now try to recall a sound you have heard that was so soothing to your ears that it made you smile and close your eyes to fully appreciate. Perhaps it was the magnificence of nature, or a symphony, or maybe a child calling home just to tell you of their love. Whatever it is, the most wonderful thing your eyes and ears have experienced will not compare to what our loving Father has in store. Just as we want the best for our children, our infinite creator God wants the very best for us, and while we are limited in what we can give our children, He is not. So we are assured by the apostle Paul, who was caught up to the third heaven (2 Cor. 12:1-4), "that which has not entered the heart of man" awaits.

While we cannot fully comprehend what God has prepared for us, we do have a brief description of our eternal dwelling. The new earth will be a gigantic land mass, having no sea at all (Rev. 21:1). During the MILLENNIUM, the heavenly Jerusalem will hover *over* the earth, but the New Jerusalem will descend all the way *to* the earth in the place where Jerusalem is today. It will be a literal, eternal city, having the squared dimensions of a cube, 1500 miles in length, width, and height (Rev. 21:16). Look at a map of the United States. The city's dimension will cover an area from Seattle to Minneapolis, down to Houston, and over to Los Angeles, though the distance from L.A. to Seattle falls short some 400 miles. That is an enormous city, and it goes up into the sky 1500 miles as well. No doubt it is that of which Jesus spoke when He said, "In My Father's house are many mansions...I go to prepare a place for you" (John 14:2).

The wall surrounding the New Jerusalem is equally staggering to the imagination. It will be 24 feet high and made of jasper, a green-colored stone which is described as "crystal clear" (Rev. 21:11, 17, 18). It will have twelve foundations made of precious stones, each foundation bearing the name of one of the twelve apostles (Rev. 21:14, 19, 20). The wall will have twelve gates, three in each direction of the compass (Rev. 21:12-13). Each gate will be made of a single pearl, each bearing the name of one of the twelve tribes of Israel (Rev. 21:12, 21), and angels will be stationed at all twelve of the gates (Rev. 21:12).

There will be no temple in the New Jerusalem, "for the Lord God, the Almighty, and the Lamb, are its temple" (Rev. 21:22). There will be "no need of the sun or of the moon to shine upon it, for the glory of God will illumine it, and its lamp is the Lamb" (Rev. 21:23).

The street of the eternal city will be pure gold, "like transparent glass" (Rev. 21:21). And in the middle of the street, the crystal clear river of the water of life will flow from the "throne of God and of the Lamb" (Rev. 22:1-2). And on either side of the river will be the tree of life, bearing twelve kinds of fruit every month (Rev. 22:2).

At that point and forever more, God will dwell among men, and "we shall see Him just as He is" (1 John 3:2). There will be no more tears, no more death, no more mourning, no more crying, and no more pain (Rev. 21:4). And for that, I joyfully shout hallelujah and praise to our glorious Lord God on high! Yes, "I will praise Thy name forever and ever" (Ps. 145:2).

> *I am the Way, and the Truth, and the Life; no one comes to the Father, but through Me.*
>
> John 14:6

Chapter 10

One Way Out...One Way In

Please pay close attention. Jesus is on the verge of receiving unto Himself His bride, the Church. When He does, all who are left behind will suffer the horrors of the Tribulation. For those who would like to avoid this hellish nightmare, there is only one way out. For those who want to behold God and dwell with Him in His glorious eternal kingdom, there is only one way in. Both ways are the same, and that is through the Lord Jesus Christ. Jesus said, "I am the Way, and the Truth, and the Life; no one comes to the Father, but through Me" (John 14:6).

In its simplest form, here is the story of man's separation from God. When God created Adam and Eve, He set them in a perfect environment in the Garden of Eden. He told them they could eat freely of any tree in the garden, except the tree of the knowledge of good and evil, that if they ate of this tree, they would surely die. Satan, the liar and destroyer, tempted Eve, offering her fruit from the very tree of which God told them they could not eat. He twisted God's words, as he always does, and Eve took of the fruit, ate it, and encouraged Adam to do so as well (see Gen. 2-3).

This act was in direct disobedience to what God had instructed, and it was the first sin ever committed by man. God walked and talked with Adam and Eve in a perfect, sinless environment, but when they disobeyed Him, they fell from God and sin wedged between God and man. God is absolute holiness, and He cannot be in the presence of sin, not because He would rather not be, but because He cannot be. Adam and Eve became the embodiment of sin for all of mankind. Scripture says, "Not one of us lives for himself" (Rom. 14:7). So as a result of their actions, every human being born thereafter is born into a sin nature, "and the wages of sin is death" (Rom. 6:23). Scripture says, "Through one man sin entered into the world, and death through sin, and so death spread to all men" (Rom. 5:12).

After Adam and Eve sinned, they were cast out of the garden to prevent them from continuing to eat of the tree of life. Had they done so, they would have lived forever in their sinful condition, and there would have been no means of reconciliation to God. Even though God knew we would sin, He created us with a free will; the ability to make our own decisions. He could have stopped them, but He allowed it because by His very nature, He will not coerce our will. But even before the sin was ever committed, God had a plan for our redemption.

Scripture says, "All things are cleansed with blood, and without shedding of blood there is no forgiveness" (Heb. 9:22). So for thousands of years while the Messianic lineage was borne out, our guilt was symbolicly transferred to an innocent substitute through faith. Every year, the high priest would enter the Temple and sacrifice a perfect, unblemished lamb as an acceptable offering to God for the sins of the people.

Then came the time for the birth of Jesus, the Savior of the world. Because of God's incomprehensible love for mankind, Jesus left His adored Father in heaven and came into the world through a virgin (Matt. 1:18-25; Luke 1:26-38) specifically and only to pay the price for man's sin once and for all (Heb. 7:27; 10:10). It was the greatest act of love mankind would ever know.

Animal sacrifices were no longer an acceptable atonement to God for sin. But in fact, "He made Him who knew no sin to be sin on our behalf, that we might become the righteousness of God in Him" (2 Cor. 5:21). The Father placed man's sin on Jesus as the perfect, unblemished Lamb of God, and He willingly went to the Cross and died (1 Pet. 1:18-19; 2:24). His death paid the price for mankind's sin forevermore. "It is a trustworthy statement, deserving full acceptance, that Christ Jesus came into the world to save sinners" (1 Tim. 1:15). And now man is reconciled to God through Him.

Scripture says, "There is salvation in no one else; for there is no other name under heaven that has been given among men, by which we must be saved" (Acts 4:12). If you have not received Jesus Christ, you must stop believing Satan's lies that you are going to heaven when you die because you are not.

Likewise, do not believe Satan's lies that you are going to heaven because you are a good person. You will not. Scripture says, "There is none good, not even one," and that "all have sinned and fall short of the glory of God" (Rom. 3:12, 23). In fact, on our very best day, God says our righteousness is as filthy rags (Isa. 64:6). Being good will not get you to heaven. I cannot stress that enough. Your eternal destination has absolutely nothing to do with being good.

It is ONLY by faith that we are saved. "Therefore having been justified by faith, we have peace with God through our Lord Jesus Christ" (Rom. 5:1). Scripture says, "For by grace you have been saved through faith; and that not of yourselves, it is the gift of God; not as a result of works, that no one should boast" (Eph. 2:8-9). And "if it is by grace, it is no longer on the basis of works, otherwise grace is no longer grace" (Rom. 11:6). By its very definition, "grace" means unmerited favor. So you cannot work your way into heaven by doing a single thing. Salvation is free, *totally free.* Scripture says, "The free gift of God is eternal life in Christ Jesus our Lord" (Rom. 6:23). We cannot *do* anything to receive it except believe in Jesus Christ and what He did for us on the Cross. "He Himself bore our sins in His body on the cross, that we might die to sin and live to righteousness; for by His wounds you were healed" (1 Pet. 2:24).

Do you want salvation? It is available to anyone who wants it. Jesus said, "Behold, I stand at the door and knock; if anyone hears My voice and opens the door, I will come in to him, and will dine with him, and he with Me" (Rev. 3:20). All you have to do is open the door and let Him in, and you must be willing to turn from sin. It is that simple. Satan is the one who has complicated the process and muddied the waters so much with his lies that people find it hard to believe that is all there is to it. I did not say you must not sin again; I said you must be willing to turn from your sin. Believe me, you will still sin from the day you receive the Lord Jesus into your life until the day you stand before Him in glory, but your sins are forgiven.

Remember, bloodshed is the only acceptable atonement for sin. When we accept Jesus as our Lord and Savior,

His blood cleanses us from our unrighteousness in the sight of God. Our sins are completely forgiven. Scripture says, "Through His name everyone who believes in Him receives forgiveness of sins" (Acts 10:43). Those committed in the past, present, and future are remembered no more (Heb. 8:12; 10:17). Our transgressions are removed from us as far as the east is from the west (Ps. 103:12). They are nailed to the Cross (Col. 2:13-14). At that point, all God sees when He looks at you and me is Christ Jesus living on the inside of us.

Really, think about it. Why would God make salvation any more difficult than simply repenting and believing in Jesus? He loves His creation. God wants us to spend eternity with Him, but that is only possible through His Son. "For God so loved the world, that He gave His only begotten Son, that whoever believes in Him should not perish, but have eternal life. For God did not send the Son into the world to judge the world, but that the world should be saved through Him" (John 3:16-17). And "God our Savior...desires all men to be saved and to come to the knowledge of the truth. For there is one God, and one mediator also between God and men...Christ Jesus" (1 Tim. 2:3-5).

So I ask you again. Do you want eternal life? Do you want a way out of the coming Tribulation? Do you want a way into the eternal kingdom? If you do, then get on your knees right now and pray this prayer out loud and from a sincere heart:

The Sinner's Prayer

Dear Lord Jesus,

I realize I am a sinner whose sins can only be forgiven by the blood You shed for me that day on Calvary. Oh, Lord, I know and believe with all of my heart that You came into this world through a virgin, lived a sinless life, and after You were crucified, God raised You from the dead and seated You at His right hand. Lord, I want You to come into my life and take up residence in my heart. I am willing to turn from sin and place all my trust in You. Jesus, thank You for paying the price for my sin. Thank You that if I were the only one to be lost, You would have still come and died just for me.

In Your precious name I pray.

Amen.

Scripture says, "If you confess with your mouth Jesus as Lord, and believe in your heart that God raised Him from the dead, you shall be saved; for with the heart man believes, resulting in righteousness, and with the mouth he confesses, resulting in salvation" (Rom. 10:9-10). If you prayed that prayer from a sincere heart, Jesus came to take up residence within you. You have been sealed "in Him with the Holy Spirit of promise, who is given as a pledge of our inheritance, with a view to the redemption of God's own possession, to the praise of His glory" (Eph. 1:13-14). In other words, you are sealed until God calls you home to glory (John 14:16-17; 2 Cor. 1:22; Eph. 4:30). You can *never* lose your salvation. And *do not let Satan convince you otherwise,* because he is going to try.

God will begin the work of perfecting you "until the day of Christ Jesus" (Phil. 1:6). It is a very slow process, and you are going to sin and make mistakes, and Satan will tempt you repeatedly. But *he is a liar.* In fact, Jesus called him "the father of lies" (John 8:44). If he can get you to doubt your salvation, then you will become less of a threat to him in leading others to the Lord by telling them what Jesus has done for you. When you sin, and you will, confess it, repent, and move on. Scripture says, "If we confess our sins, He is faithful and righteous to forgive us our sins and to cleanse us from all unrighteousness" (1 John 1:9). Indeed, your sins were forgiven the moment you invited Jesus into your heart, but when we sin, we also need to confess it because sin breaks the fellowship we enjoy with God.

Finally, just as you eat food to keep your body strong, you also need food to keep your Spirit strong. Scripture says, "Like newborn babes, long for the pure milk of the Word, that by it you may grow in respect to salvation" (1 Pet. 2:2). When you do not eat, you gradually weaken physically. So it is with the Spirit. You must discipline yourself to read the Bible daily and pray or else your spiritual state will gradually weaken. The importance of this daily regimen simply cannot be overstated. Find a Bible-teaching church where you can plant your roots and grow with the body of Christ. In a forest, you never see one tree toppled over with its roots pulled out of the ground because the roots are all intertwined. In the same way, the body of Christ will help strengthen you against the enemy so you will stand strong in the storms of life.

A Pastor's Prayer

Heavenly Father,

I pray Your hedge of protection around these new baby believers. I ask that You bind the attacks of discouragement and doubt. Lord, will You open their eyes and their hearts so they may know You and the power of Your Word in their lives. Father, send people who will surround them and help them grow spiritually in the knowledge of who You are. Lord God, I ask that You give them a passionate heart to follow You in all of Your glorious ways. And, Father, I pray that You enable them to trust You implicitly.

Lord, I ask all these things in Jesus' name.

Amen.

Let me be the first to welcome you to the eternal family as my new brother or sister in Christ. Our Lord Jesus said, "I tell you, there is joy in the presence of the angels of God over one sinner who repents" (Luke 15:10). Just think of it, the Lord and the angels and all the children of God in His presence are rejoicing right now over the decision you just made, and I am delighted as well that we will be spending eternity together with our glorious Lord God. I look forward to seeing you there!

Dr. John R. Bisagno